And Not A Shot is Fired

Dombrowski

The publisher gratefully acknowledges
the generous contribution of
The MacPherson Charitable Trust,
which helped to make
this RWU Press edition of
And Not a Shot Is Fired
a reality.

AND NOT A SHOT IS FIRED

by

JAN KOZAK

(Member of the Secretariat of the Communist Party of Czechoslovakia)

RWU PRESS
Robert Welch University Press

Robert Welch University Press

Appleton, Wisconson

1999

New 1999 edition with
foreword by Thomas R. Eddlem
and index
not in the original.

Originally published in Czech under the title:
How Parliament Can Play a Revolutionary Part in the Transition to Socialism and the Role of the Popular Masses

Published by
Robert Welch University Press
P.O. Box 8050
Appleton, Wisconsin 54913

RWU PRESS
Robert Welch University Press

Printed in the United States of America
Library of Congress Catalog Card Number: 99-071272
ISBN: 1-892647-01-X

Introduction

ONE MIGHT ask today, years after the fall of the Berlin Wall: "Why would anyone want to read a report by a communist about the revolutionary takeover of Czechoslovakia — a country that no longer exists? The Czechs are capitalists now, remember?"

Such a question reveals a number of erroneous assumptions that this document convincingly refutes — not the least of which is the false assumption that the leaders of the former Communist states of Eastern Europe were wedded to ideology. As Jan Kozak and 40 years of brutal Communist Party rule in Czechoslovakia so clearly demonstrate, communism was a *tactic* employed for the assumption of power, rather than a sincere belief. These same tactics, modified only slightly, are being used today. Americans who labor under the false premise that communism is either an ideology or a system of economics that died with the Cold War do so at their personal and national peril.

Most Americans are falsely conditioned to believe today that elective governments are permanently established and practically invincible to destruction, so long as elections are free from fraud and consumers can buy Big Mac hamburgers in the market. *And Not a Shot Is Fired* authoritatively disproves that myth. This document is a "how-to" manual for totalitarian takeover of an elected parliamentary system of government through mainly *legal* and *constitutional* means. Kozak did not pontificate fuzzy theories of how "revolutionary parliamentarianism" *might* be accomplished. He wrote from personal experience and intimate knowledge of how this seizure of power *actually was accomplished*. Kozak's manual is especially important for contemporary Americans because most of the same methods described in this book are at work in the United States today, although those methods are not being followed directly under communist ideological auspices. More on that, after a little background.

Origin of the Document

And Not A Shot Is Fired only accidentally made it into the public domain. Written between 1950 and 1955 (and revised somewhat after that) as an internal Czechoslovak Communist Party strategy paper, the two chapters which comprise this document were discussed briefly by Communist Czechoslovak delegates to the Inter-Parliamentary Union (IPU) in London in the fall of 1957. Kozak was a member of the Czechoslovak Communist Party Central Committee, briefly a member of the government secretariat, and later, official historian for the Czechoslovak Communist Party. A copy of these two chapters, officially entitled *How Parliament Can Play a Revolutionary Part in the Transition to Socialism* and *The Role of the Popular Masses*, were requested through IPU channels by British delegates to the conference. The word came back from the Czechoslovaks that the just-published manuscript was mysteriously "out of print." It was not until January of 1961 that, according to the original British publishers, "by a mere coincidence, a copy of the report was secured." [1]

Once received, Kozak's manifesto was quickly translated into English and published in February of that year by London's Independent Research Centre under a combination of the titles Kozak had given them: *How Parliament Can Play a Revolutionary Part in the Transition to Socialism and the Role of the Popular Masses*. The document became an instant international sensation, and by the beginning of 1962 Kozak's manual was being widely distributed in several languages throughout Europe and the United States. Radio Free Europe (RFE) published its own English translation under the original title, and a committee of Congress reproduced and distributed the RFE translation as well. It is the RFE translation (as published by Congress) which we have reproduced here.

But most Americans who came to know Jan Kozak and his step-by-step program for a totalitarian takeover of a free government read the book under the title *And Not A Shot Is Fired*, under which the Connecticut-based Long House publishers distributed the original British translation of Kozak's manual. The title of the popular American edition came straight out of the superb introduction by John Howland Snow. Snow explained that Kozak's document is a blueprint of how a "representative government can be made authoritarian, legally, piece by piece. The form remains, an empty shell.... And not a shot is fired." [2]

Americans with only a little knowledge of post-war Europe are under the illusion that after the defeat of Hitler, Stalin installed his lackeys in Eastern European governments solely by force of the Soviet Army. This was not the case. Stalin had to pledge at least the appearance of free elections at Yalta, even if the concessions granted by Franklin D. Roosevelt guaranteed the eventual absorption of Eastern Europe into Stalin's orbit. Eastern Europe actually enjoyed a short period of relative freedom after the war, during 1946 and 1947, when there were more or less free elections. Most of the Soviet-occupied countries elected non-communist majorities, despite severe harassment of non-communist parties during the election campaigns. This document explains how, after the elections in Czechoslovakia, the Communist Party insinuated itself into a coalition with Social Democrats and gained control of the Agricultural and Interior ministries.

The value of this book is not that it explained "new" techniques or strategies for taking over free governments. There was nothing original in the strategies and tactics for taking over free governments outlined by Kozak, although many Americans in the 1960s — even among those who thought they were well informed — regarded Kozak's blueprint as new tactics and ideology. In fact, most of what Kozak describes had been theorized a generation earlier by Italian Communist Party chief Antonio Gramsci. But only Kozak has demonstrated how such a takeover actually was accomplished. *And Not A Shot Is Fired* has enduring value for several reasons, not the least of which is that the brief treatise is sufficiently straightforward — and comparatively free of communistic dialectical jargon — that it can be profitably read by the casual reader. That the document was written in a form readily comprehensible by the lay reader can only be chalked up to Communist overconfidence in the inevitable ascendancy of their empire. Kozak boasted that the Communist empire "comprises over 25 per cent of the whole world; 35 per cent of the world's population lives in it and about 30 per cent of the world's industrial output is produced by it." (Page 1) To be sure, Jan Kozak prolifically used communistic patois throughout the manual, drawing from a lexicon that has been alternatively termed "dialectics," "wordsmanship," and "Aesopean language." And the document can be read much more profitably with a thorough knowledge of the Communist Party's dialectic of that time frame. But Kozak's manuscript is one of those rare specimens of totalitarian literature where the main thrust of the document is understandable on its face even without that knowledge.

Ideology as a Tactic, Not a Belief

The one, overriding goal stressed by Kozak was the objective of seizing total power. There is no concern for the lot of the poor, or the conditions of the laborer, or even the wealth of the industrialist evident in this manuscript; power is the one and only goal:

> The overall character of the participation in this government was: not to lose sight, even for a moment, the carrying out of a complete socialist coup. (Page 12)
>
> By using these methods, this principle was fulfilled in practice: not to lose sight for a single moment of the aim of a complete socialist overthrow. (Page 18)
>
> [T]he following may and must be carried out successfully ... concentration of all power in the hands of the [communist-dominated] parliament." (Page 38)
>
> In the course of the fight for the complete takeover of all power... (Page 39)
>
> Its [the Communist Party's] aim was ... the definite settlement of the question of power by consolidating people's democracy into a state of the dictatorship of the proletariat. (Page 46)

There are more passages in the book about how the leaders of the Czechoslovak Communist Party sought dictatorial power for themselves, but the murderous 40-year reign of this criminal syndicate (a criminal syndicate clothed with the pretended legitimacy of state power) makes further elucidation unnecessary. Kozak was no dreamy-eyed professor embracing a nebulous idea of a future socialist utopia; he and his confederates were reality-hardened schemers who would use any method available to gain as much power as possible. To power-hungry conspirators like Kozak, Communist ideology was mainly a useful cover for the organizational undertaking of a *coup d'etat* — a tactic, not a belief system. The Communists actually disdained other socialists, such as social democrats, even though they constantly strove to coalesce with and co-opt these democratic parties.

Co-opting Ideological Language

The Communists adapted the language of socialist ideology and the political policies of socialist regimes for their own internal use on several fronts. Many socialist terms were given double meanings — sometimes called "dialectics" — among Communist revolutionaries for furtherance of their coup. Thus, terms like "proletariat" and "worker's class" can have their plain meaning or be code words for "Communist Party leaders." Or, "people's interest," "democratic will of the masses" and "decision of the proletariat" could have its ordinary meaning or designate "orders from Party leadership."

The use of dialectic meaning in words was and remains a necessary part of any plan to overthrow free governments. Outright announcement of the goals and motivations of revolutionaries would arouse too much alarm among the people and create too much resistance, resulting in the defeat of the conspirators. The use of such double-meaning terms serves as a means of transmitting, indirectly, an action program to fellow conspirators without alarming the general populace. If confronted with the true dialectical meaning of the terms, conspirators can simply claim that it is merely ideological belief, and that the accuser is simply a paranoid who is falsely reading sinister motivations into the revolutionary's words.

Dialectical speech was not unique to Kozak's Czechoslovak branch of the Communist Party, nor has it been limited to Communism. Mafiosi and other criminal gangs typically have their own language that serves both as verbal handshakes and to communicate without attracting the notice of the law. And like the lingo of gangsters, Communist dialectics changes frequently in order to preserve its esoteric qualities. (Few would think that "wise guys" today would utilize antiquated terms such as "rubbed out," "greased," or "squeezed" anymore, because they have long been in the common parlance.)

In Communist history, dialectical "code-speech" goes all the way back to the beginning. As far back as 1848, when Karl Marx and Friedrich Engels completed *The Communist Manifesto*, it was widely condemned as being a conspiratorial document. Few literate men then took seriously Marx and Engels' preposterous claim that the government-power grab which comprised the ten-plank platform in *The Communist Manifesto* would lead to what the two later promised as the "withering away" of the state.[3] To claim that the state withers away when you give it more power requires profound stupidity or brazen dishonesty. And, by all accounts, Marx and Engels were not stupid. *The Communist Manifesto*, like Kozak's manuscript, is simply a manual of how to take control of a government, the latter having laid out the scheme in both more openly brazen terms and greater mechanical detail.

Tactical "Ideology" for Would-Be Dictators: Socialism

To a Communist conspirator like Kozak, socialist ideology offered advantages beyond mere discreet communication with fellow revolutionaries. Revolutionaries frequently promote socialism because a socialist economy — even socialism under a parliamentary system of government — heavily concentrates power in the hands of the few people who run the state. Concentration of power in the hands of a few government leaders makes the state easier to seize by a determined conspiracy. To conspirators, socialism serves as a control-the-wealth program, not a share-the-wealth program. Thus, none should be surprised that Hitler and Mussolini took over freely-elected parliaments in their countries — legally and constitutionally, as Kozak and his co-conspirators later accomplished — only after posing as socialist ideologues of one form or another.

Some may contest the assertion that Hitler and Mussolini arose out of socialism because of popular notions that these dictators stem from the "right" wing of the ideological spectrum. Such illusions have no basis in fact. The very name "Nazi" was almost never used by the Nazis themselves; it was merely an acronym for Hitler's "National Socialist Party" which created such socialist institutions as the government automobile industry. (Volkswagen, which originated as a government program under the Hitler regime, means "people's car" in German.) And Mussolini's deep socialist roots date back to before World War I, with his editorship of the socialist newspaper, *Avanti!* From a power politics perspective Mussolini's fascism, after being imposed upon Italy, differed only superficially with outright socialism. Mussolini had completely adopted the notion that government should be fully involved in controlling property, even if he did allow nominal private ownership. *Il Duce*'s program that the state would be the "supreme regulator of the relations between all citizens of the state"[4] fits hand-in-glove with the political program instituted by Kozak and his co-conspirators after they had taken power for themselves. Economic fascism, which is simply heavy government regulation and control of what is only nominally private property, serves essentially the same purpose for conspirators as outright government ownership under socialism. And fascism is the economic program increasingly being followed in the United States and the formerly socialist nations of Eastern Europe today. Economic fascism offers a number of advantages for the modern conspirator over the socialism used by Kozak — but only because fascism is typically called some other nebulous name such as "Third Way" or "public-private partnership," or (even worse) falsely represented as "privatization," or "free trade," or "free enterprise." The fascist economic model does not carry all the public relations baggage of Stalinist socialism, and, over the short term at least, it can be more economically efficient than outright socialism.* Thus, it should be no surprise that the same conspirators who ran the governments of former Soviet "Republics" of Eastern Europe have readily exchanged their Communist Party posts for "elective" posts, or that the brand of state control they are now pushing is called "privatization" and "economic reform."

Pressure from Above, Pressure from Below

A socialist or fascist economic policy is necessary for dictatorial revolution in an elective government — and not simply because socialism or fascism concentrates the physical power of the state in the few who run the executive branch of government. While these policies certainly enable the state to acquire

---

*Under fascism, the "private" property owner may be heavily controlled by government rules and regulations, but he is often still under the illusion that he "owns" his property. Thus, he may still strive to improve his property as a property owner would in a *laissez-faire* system. This is particularly the case when the fascist state, in its benevolence, *allows* the propertied class to keep some of its wealth or to make some decisions (within government guidelines, of course).

power (and to shift power away from the legislature) their chief role as necessary ingredients for revolution is that they give the state hegemonic control (leadership) over the various *non-governmental* cultural institutions — institutions which may have enough strength to resist and overthrow a political *coup d'etat*. Kozak uses an excellent example in this text of the hegemonic leadership manufactured by the Communists over agriculture in Czechoslovakia. Farmers and ranchers have traditionally been very conservative, independent, and resistant to tyranny. In a heavily agricultural state such as war-devastated Czechoslovakia, farmers and ranchers would have been a strong counter-revolutionary force. Indeed, Stalin had found farmers to be the chief anti-totalitarian force in pre-war Ukraine.

But in Czechoslovakia, Communist cadres "from below" infiltrated and co-opted the conservative leadership of the agricultural interests, giving the misleading impression that farmers were divided on the revolution — or perhaps even supportive of it. Meanwhile, "parliamentary socialism" — the "pressure from above" — used the power of the state, under the pretext of yielding to pressure from "farmers" (represented by these Communist infiltrators) to break up the economic base and strength of the independent farmers.

As the preceding example illustrates, Kozak outlined the main thesis of a giant pincer's strategy for transforming a parliamentary system of government into a totalitarian dictatorship — the strategy of combining "pressure from above" with "pressure from below" to effect revolutionary change. In essence, under this plan, the Communist minority in parliament (in coalition with socialist parties) serves the revolution by initiating policies and legislation which strengthen the hand of grassroots revolutionaries and punish threats to the coup (i.e., the Right). Meanwhile, grassroots revolutionaries whip up the appearance of popular support for the legislative program to advance the revolution through strikes, rallies, petitions, threats, and — sometimes — sabotage. The "pressure from below" by the small number of revolutionaries and their larger number of dupes is then used to "justify" the centralization of power in the hands of the executive branch of the state. Wishy-washy politicians are intimidated, and the "pressure from above" intensifies. Each legislative victory results in new demands (the "pressure from below") for even stronger legislation, which is relentlessly pursued by communists and their dupes in parliament — who claim, of course, that they are acting in the name of the popular will. The cycle continues until opposition is completely powerless, intimidated, or liquidated — and the revolution is a *fait accompli.*

The theory for using "pressure from above" and "pressure from below" in order to acquire power, explained in this manual by Kozak, first emerged in the writings of an obscure Italian Communist thinker named Antonio Gramsci. Gramsci had plenty of time for contemplating the reasons why his Communist Party had lost Italy to Benito Mussolini, since he spent the last years of his life in Mussolini's jails. Gramsci concluded that in order to capture the power in a state, one must first capture the culture. By culture, Gramsci meant the powerful non-governmental institutions of great influence throughout the nation, specifically: churches, unions, mass media, political parties, universities and educational centers, business organizations, foundations, etc. Gramsci explained that, in hindsight, it was unreasonable to expect the Communists to have seized power in pre-World War II Italy in the same way that the October Revolution had succeeded in Russia. "In [totalitarian, Tsarist] Russia the state was everything," Gramsci explained in his *Prison Notebooks*. "[C]ivil society was primordial and gelatinous; in the West, there was a proper relation between state and civil society, and when the state trembled a sturdy structure of civil society was at once revealed."[5]

In the West, Gramsci explained, family loyalties, faith in God, and lawful limits on governmental power were thoroughly represented in the cultural institutions. Gramsci wrote that "there can and must be a 'political hegemony' even before assuming government power, and in order to exercise political leadership or hegemony one must not count solely on the power and material force that is given by government."[6] Gramsci argued that without a successful "war of position" for "cultural hegemony" (cultural leadership) within these institutions, a revolutionary power grab — even by a well-organized conspiracy — is impossible. Ultimately, the Italian Communists were outmaneuvered in the cultural war by Mussolini's blackshirts. Belief in God, family, and limited government in the developed nations of the West constitutes a cultural system of "fortresses and earthworks" against revolution, according to Gramsci. A *coup d'etat*, without having first subverted these "fortresses and earthworks" through the acquisition of political/cultural hegemony, would only be temporary and result in a quick and successful counter revolution. The revolutionaries of today are well aware that their struggle for control of the culture cannot be won overnight. Gramsci follower and Frankfort school of socialism apostle Rudi Dutschke explained the Gramscian struggle as a "long march through the institutions"[7] to win Gramsci's "war of position" over any cultural institutions which would stand in the way of a *coup d'etat* by a conspiratorial faction.

To revolutionaries like Kozak and Gramsci, all cultural and governmental institutions constitute battlefields. Kozak explained that the Czech Communist Party created "mass organizations" to form that pressure from below, and used the power of the state to take over, eliminate or isolate the old conservative institutions: "[T]he 'pressure from above' was applied in an ever-increasing measure for the direct suppression and destruction of the counter-revolutionary machinations of the bourgeoisie [the middle class]. Let us recall the signal role played in the development and extension of that pressure by the Ministry of the Interior, for instance, which was led by the Communists and the units of the State Security directed by them." (Page 13) As the state passed draconian gun control laws throughout Eastern European countries in the aftermath of World War II, the Communist Party armed itself and — together with its control of the police organs of government — obtained a monopoly on force in these nations. "The necessity of arming the most mature part of the workers' class for repulsing the counter-revolutionary machinations of the bourgeoisie ... has been proved, incidentally, again by the later formation of the workers' militias in peoples' democratic Hungary and Poland," Kozak emphasized. (Page 25) That victorious revolutionaries would need a monopoly on force to consolidate control of a country is an obvious necessity, and it highlights our Second Amendment-protected right to keep and bear arms as an obvious "earthwork" against revolution. But in Czechoslovakia, it should be emphasized, the monopoly on force mainly served a more subtle purpose than a violent overthrow; it created a helpless feeling among the increasingly isolated non-communist opposition. The clash of arms was never necessary.

Many elements of the "pressure from above" and "pressure from below" stratagem explained by Kozak are being used against Americans on a variety of fronts toward the consolidation of power in the hands of the state. Kozak explained that the revolution also "breaks through the onerous circle of intimidation and spiritual terror of the old institutions, the Church, etc." (Page 19) Modern activists and would-be revolutionaries attempt to isolate and outmaneuver those churches that cling to traditional teachings by (for example) using Kozak's tactics to effect change on the issue of birth control and abortion. Both the U.S. government and the United Nations (as well as tax-exempt foundations) fund private organizations such as Planned Parenthood that perform abortions and distribute birth control devices. At the same time, these organizations lobby governments and create the appearance of popular support for government-subsidized abortion on demand and (eventually) coercive population-control programs. The United Nations uses a Non-Governmental Organization (NGO) caucus of left-wing organizations to create grassroots (pressure from below) to justify its authoritarian agenda, which (on the population-control front) includes support for China's population-control program of forced abortion. The NGOs, of course, by no means represent the grassroots. But that does not prevent the movers and shakers at the top — including the foundation heads and governmental officials who lavishly fund them — from representing them as such. There are dozens of other modern examples of how the "pressure from above" has created and funded the "pressure from below," from the environmentalist movement to the international gun control movement, the details of which could fill many pages.

The U.S. Constitution — a formidable "earthwork"

The U.S. Constitution — by way of contrast with parliamentary socialism/fascism — offers a formidable series of barriers to would-be dictators, with its separation of powers, system of checks and balances, reserved rights, delegated powers, and free enterprise-based economy. James Madison explained in *The Federalist,* #47, that the division of powers in the U.S. Constitution was devised with the following guiding principle of politics constantly in mind: "The accumulation of all powers, legislative, executive, and judiciary, in the same hands, whether of one, a few, or many, and whether hereditary, self-appointed, or elective, may justly be pronounced the very definition of tyranny."

Gramsci strongly felt that "the whole liberal [i.e., classical, laissez-faire liberalism] ideology, with its strengths and weaknesses, can be summed up in the principle of the division of powers, and the source of liberalism's weakness becomes apparent: it is the bureaucracy, i.e. the crystallization of the leading personnel, which exercises coercive power..."[8] In other words, Gramsci was saying that revolutionaries can make use of ambitious individual politicians — who need not necessarily be revolutionaries at first — to usurp power and break down the division of powers which limits government in constitutional systems. Madison concurred in *The Federalist*, #10, that the main problem in free governments was the tendency to faction and ambition among the ruling personalities. "The friend of popular governments never finds himself so much alarmed for their character and fate as when he contemplates their propensity to this dangerous vice," the Father of the Constitution explained. But the Founders constructed the U.S. Constitution to ameliorate this very problem. As Alexander Hamilton explained in *The Federalist*, #9:

> The regular distribution of power into distinct departments; the introduction of legislative balances and checks; the institution of courts composed of judges holding their offices during good behavior; the representation of the

people in the legislature by deputies of their own election: these are wholly new discoveries, or have made their principal progress towards perfection in modern times. They are means, and powerful means, by which the excellencies of republican government may be retained and its imperfections lessened or avoided.

What Can Be Done?

To a large extent, many of our cultural and governmental institutions have already been captured by forces in favor of the centralization of government power and, opposed to limited government and the traditional morality of the churches. Few Americans are even aware that an invasion of our institutions has been ongoing — or that the invaders have won several engagements. Author and political commentator John T. Flynn has already been proven partly right in his 1941 warning that "We will not recognize [American totalitarianism] as it rises. It will wear no black shirts here. It will probably have no marching songs. It will rise out of a congealing of a group of elements that exist here and that are the essential components of Fascism.... It will be at first decorous, humane, glowing with homely American sentiment."[9] Several of the constitutional "fortresses and earthworks" which the Founding Fathers threw up to block revolution in our constitutional system have given way to decay in recent decades. The marginalization of gun ownership through federal legislation, the progressive lack of respect for the federal system of states rights by both political parties, and the assault on free speech rights protected by the First Amendment through so-called "campaign finance reform" are but a few of many examples. Part of the "long march through the institutions" has already been completed.

But it is not yet too late. There are still cultural and structural layers of "fortresses and earthworks" which continue to protect Americans against the kind of quasi-legal revolution this book outlines. There are still some checks and balances and division of powers left in our system, and there is still vigorous organizational opposition to consolidation of governmental powers. But these defenses are under siege. The only way to guarantee continued free government is for Americans to get active in restoring those political and cultural "fortresses and earthworks" which support the principles James Madison and the rest of the founders put into the U.S. Constitution. We can guard this principle of the division of powers by insisting — both directly and especially through those cultural institutions where we can have any influence — that our elected officials revive the separation of powers and consistently vote for a reduction in the size and scope of government.

Thomas R. Eddlem
Appleton, WI
January 1999

Endnotes to the Introduction

[1]Lord Morrison of Lambeth, Introduction to *How Parliament Can Play a Revolutionary Part in the Transition to Socialism and the Role of the Popular Masses* (London: Independent Information Centre, 1961), 9th edition, pp. 3-4.
[2] John Howland Snow, Introduction to *And Not a Shot Is Fired* (New Caanan, CT: The Long House, Inc., 1972), pp. 8-9.
[3] See, for example, Engels in 1878: Frederick Engels, *Herr Eugen Dühring's Revolution in Science* (New York: International Publishers, 1939), p. 307. Also, Marx was on record having said much the same thing in his 1875 "Critique of the Gotha Program": *Karl Marx: Selected Writings in Sociology & Social Philosophy*, (New York: McGraw-Hill, 1964), p. 256.
[4] Benito Mussolini, *My Autobiography* (New York: Charles Scribner's Sons, 1928) p. 280.

[5] Roger Simon, *Gramsci's Political Thought* (London: Lawrence and Wishart, 1982), p. 28.
[6] Antonio Gramsci, *Prison Notebooks, Volume I* (New York: Columbia University Press, 1992), p.137.
[7] Richard Grenier, *Capturing the Culture* (Washington, DC: Ethics and Public Policy Center, 1991), p. xlv.
[8] Antonio Gramsci, *The Modern Prince and Other Writings* (New York: International Publishers, 1959), p.186.
[9] John T. Flynn, "Coming: A Totalitarian America" (originally appearing in the February 1941 *American Mercury),* in *Forgotton Lessons* (Irvington-on-Hudson, NY: Foundation for Economic Education, 1996), pp. 142-143.

And Not a Shot Is Fired

How Parliament Can Play a Revolutionary Part in the Transition to Socialism
and
The Role of the Popular Masses

by Jan Kozak

Translated from the original Czech

Publisher's note: *This document was originally published in the Czech language, and the following is an exact replication of the translation from the U.S. government's Radio Free Europe and published by the House Committee on Un-American Activities of the 87th Congress. For the purposes of clarity and better readability, we have added subheadings, changed italics, and adjusted arbitrary spaces between paragraphs.*

How Parliament Can Play a Revolutionary Part in the Transition to Socialism and The Role of the Popular Masses

by Jan Kozak

THE classics of Marxism-Leninism never ceased to point out that the inexorable revolutionary transformation of the capitalist society into a socialist one does not preclude, but even presupposes the possibility of various forms and roads of the proletarian revolution. V. I. Lenin, in particular, illuminated this serious question thoroughly and systematically. In his lifetime the proletarian revolution became an immediate question of the day. In his theoretical works and concretely in his practical activity he started from the principle that the forms of transition to socialism are dependent on the concrete balance of international and internal class forces, on the degree of organization of the proletariat and the bourgeoisie, on the ability to gain allies, the level of the economic structure and on the political traditions and forms of the organizations.

From the moment the Great Socialist October Revolution broke the chains of imperialism and gave power to the relatively weak proletariat of the nations of backward Russia, profound objective and subjective changes began to take place in the world. The present fruit of the Socialist October Revolution is the new historical era, the characteristic feature of which lies in the origin and consolidation of the socialist global constellation. This constellation now embraces 17 countries, with the USSR and China at its head; it comprises over 25 per cent of the whole world; 35 per cent of the world's population lives in it and about 30 per cent of the world's industrial output is produced by it.

The second characteristic feature of this new historical era is the collapse of the colonial system as a world factor. Important Asian and African countries such as India, Indonesia, Burma, Egypt and others have cast off the shackles of imperialism. In the interest of their further development they are obliged to cooperate with the socialist camp and thus to strike new blows at world capitalism.

Both these main characteristics of the new historical era — the origin of the socialist constellation and the collapse of the colonial system — have profoundly changed the objective structure of the world. These profound changes in the objective structure of the world are necessarily accompanied also by profound subjective changes — changes in the thinking, views, political and practical orientation of the broad popular masses. The aggravated conflicts in the weakened capitalist constellation compel the imperialists to resort to harsher oppression, exploitation, suppression of national rights, interference with democracy and preparations for a new war. By this, however, they cause broader and broader oppressed and dissatisfied social sections to rally against them, sections which are fighting against national suppression, for democracy and peace. In this struggle for national and democratic interests, the individual trends and currents of the anti-imperialist battle are forming their ranks. These trends, which are the result and the product of the new subjective processes in society, are, however, dispersed, isolated and constantly weakened by the propaganda of the ruling bourgeoisie and by the ideology and practice of reformism. In a number of capitalist and dependent countries there still slumbers the enormous, but still dispersed force of the broad popular masses. In this situation the workers' class in these countries is faced with the task of firmly taking a stand at the head of the struggle for the national and democratic interests of its respective nations, of uniting in its fight for socialism and of creating, under its leadership, a united and mighty anti-imperialist popular movement.

The new historical era and its tasks have created most favorable conditions for the workers' class in this way for gaining new allies. The old tenets about the allies of the workers' class which corresponded to old historical conditions are undergoing a change and are widening. Along with the changed conditions for the struggle for national democratic and peace interests, the conditions for the struggle of the workers' class for socialism are also changing. In the fight against imperialism, which endeavors to overcome its conflicts by completely ignoring the interests of the nations and which strives to liquidate their independence as states, the national role of the workers' class is growing and it is placed in the forefront of all patriotic and democratic forces.

Patriotism: A Difficulty for the Proletarian Revolution

"Patriotism," V. I. Lenin proclaimed, "is one of the deepest feelings firmly rooted in the hearts of people for hundreds and thousands of years from the moment their separate fatherlands began to exist. It has been one of the greatest, one can say exceptional, difficulties of our proletarian revolution that it had to pass through a period of sharpest conflict with patriotism during the time of the Brest-Litovsk peace." (V. I. Lenin, "Spisy" Vol. 28, Czech edition, 1955, p. 187.)

It is a great, one may say exceptionally favorable, circumstance for the socialist revolution in the present situation that patriotism, "one of the feelings most deeply rooted in people," leans on and needs socialism in the struggle against imperialism for national interests. In this way patriotism and democracy have become mighty weapons of the workers' class in present times and, step by step, they bring masses of new allies to the workers' class.

Parliament as "an instrument ... of the socialist revolution"

The new conditions which are the consequence of the profound objective and subjective changes in the world create also new opportunities and prospects for the socialist revolution, new avenues as far as the forms of transition to socialism are concerned. In a number of countries which are particularly weakened by the conflicts within the capitalist order, the opportunity has arisen for the workers' class to place itself firmly at the head of great popular movements for national independence, democracy, peace and socialism, to defeat the reactionary anti-people forces striving for the maintenance and aggravation of national oppression and exploitation, to win a decisive majority in parliament and to change it from an organ of the bourgeois democracy into an organ of power for the democracy of working people, into a direct instrument of power for the peaceful development of the socialist revolution.

Also, our experience provides notable and practical proof that it is possible to transform parliament from an instrument of the bourgeoisie into an instrument of the revolutionary democratic will of the people and into an instrument for the development of the socialist revolution.

When the German imperialist occupiers, aided by the treacherous bourgeoisie at home and with the consent of the Western imperialist powers, destroyed the national liberty and the independence of the Czechoslovak republic in 1938 and 1939, the Communist Party of Czechoslovakia (hereinafter CPCS) placed itself at the head of the struggle for national liberation by the Czech and Slovak people. Following up the policy of the Popular Front originating from the time of the defense of the republic against fascism at home and abroad, it formed, in the course of a heavy fight against the occupiers requiring many sacrifices, a broad National Front, in which stood, under the leadership of the workers' class, and side by side with it, peasants, tradesmen, the intelligentsia, and part of the Czech and Slovak bourgeoisie. This broad National Front, embracing all patriotic and democratic forces of the country, was led by the working class into the national and democratic revolution.

Thanks to the fact that Hitler's Germany was crushed by the armies of the Soviet Union and that our country was directly liberated by the Soviet army, that national and democratic revolution conquered. As a consequence the occupation power of the German imperialists and of their domestic helpmates — the treacherous financial, industrial and agrarian upper bourgeoisie — was swept away, national unity and independence as a state was revived and a deep-reaching democratization of the country was carried out. Furthermore, the sovereignty and independence of Czechoslovakia was renewed in the form of a new, people's democratic order.

The Communist Party Consolidates Its Influence

In this struggle the workers' class, led by the CPCS, became the recognized driving force of the nation; its action-unity was consolidated and the influence of reformism which had splintered it in the years of the pre-Munich republic was weakened. The victory of the national and democratic revolution meant for the workers' class, which had relied in this struggle on all patriotic and democratic forces — the peasants, tradesmen, the intelligentsia and part of the Czech and Slovak bourgeoisie — its access to power

The workers' class was the main force in the new revolutionary democratic government (the so-called Kosice Government) and in the national committees — the new organs of the state's power created from below by the revolutionary masses. The program for the building of the liberated republic, which had been elaborated and submitted by the Communists and which became the program of the government, was quickly implemented by the revolutionary activity of the popular masses. Its implementation gave rise to far-reaching political, economic, social and cultural changes in the country.

Of the political points in this program, these were the most important: the breaking up of the basic members of the old oppressive bourgeois state apparatus and *assumption of power by the national committees,* the formation of a new people's security system and army, *the prohibition of the revival of the political parties which had represented the treacherous upper bourgeoisie,* a systematic purge of the entire political, economic and cultural life of the country, the settlement of the relations between the Czech and Slovak nations on the principle of equality, the expulsion of the German minority, etc.

Changing the Social Structure

Of the economic measures, the following were the most important: the transfer of all enemy property, of that of the treacherous upper bourgeoisie and of other traitors, to the national administration of the new people's authority; the transfer of the land belonging to these enemies and traitors to the ownership of landless persons, tenants and working smallholders.

The principal foreign policy task was unequivocal alliance with the Soviet Union, safeguarding national liberty and independence as a state and further undisturbed, peaceful development for the nations of Czechoslovakia.

All these measures, aiming at far-reaching changes in the social structure of the country, emanated directly from the conditions and tasks of the anti-fascist, national and democratic fight for liberation and arose from the old democratic traditions and longing of our people and they, furthermore, deepened and safeguarded that democracy. One of the tasks the Czechoslovak workers' class set itself in the struggle for the national and democratic interests of the people was, also, therefore, the *re-establishment of the institution of Parliament* which the occupiers had abolished, aided by the treacherous domestic upper bourgeoisie and traditions which had deep roots among the people. As early as the end of the summer of 1945, after agreement had been reached between the political parties forming the National Front, the Provisional National Assembly was elected (on the principle of parity representation) and, in May 1946, the Constituent National Assembly in general, secret, direct and fair elections. The composition of Parliament was strongly influenced by the results of the revolution, by the practical schooling of the working masses in the course of the victorious revolution. Of the eight political parties which were part of the National Front of Czechs and Slovaks at the time of the elections, the Communist Party emerged as by far the strongest. It gained over 40 per cent of the votes in the Czech lands and, with the Communist Party of Slovakia, 38 per cent of the votes cast in the state as a whole. Parliament and, along with it, the fight between the workers' class and the bourgeoisie about its role and content, entered the history of the people's democratic development of Czechoslovakia. The workers' class, whose struggle had made it possible that this institution could be re-established, strove for Parliament, as one of the most prominent political traditions and forms of the past, to change its character (lit.: content; Tr.), to change it from an instrument of the workers' class into one of the levers actuating the further development and consolidation of the revolution, into a direct instrument for the socialist building of the country. The bourgeoisie, on the other hand, strove for Parliament to be revised with its old content — bourgeois parliamentarianism — and tried to use it for the stopping of the revolution, for the demolition of its achievements, for the consolidation and widening of its former political and economic power positions, for the preparation of the restoration of its former rule and dictatorship.

Parliament Provides "Pressure From Above"

This struggle took place during the period from 1946–1948. In the course of these years the workers' class, led by the Communists, made effective use of all its old forms of fighting, employed by the revolutionary workers' parties in Parliament, adjusted, however to the new conditions, and found new ones. Helped by Parliament, which was used by the workers' class for deepening the revolution and for the gradual, peaceful and bloodless change of the national and democratic revolution into a socialist one as "pressure from above," and by its effect on the growth of the "pressure from below," the bourgeoisie was pushed step by step from its share in the power. This gradual and bloodless driving of the bourgeoisie from power and the quite legitimate constitutional expansion of the power of the workers' class and of the working people was completed in February 1948 by the parliamentary settlement of the government crisis engineered by the bourgeoisie. The scope of power was definitely settled in favor of the workers' class, and Parliament, as one of the instruments of its power, began to serve immediately the socialist transformation of the country.

Parliament, which had played an important role in pre-Munich, capitalist Czechoslovakia in the political, economic, cultural and social life of the country, which had awakened and created a number of bourgeois, democratic, parliamentary traditions among broad sections of the population, underwent a change. *The form remained but the content was different.* Our working people, led by the Communists, provided practical proof during the years 1945-1948 that it was possible to transform parliament from an organ of the bourgeoisie into an instrument developing democratic measures of consequence, leading to the gradual change of the social structure and into a direct instrument for the victory of the socialist revolution.

From Capitalism to Socialism — By Means of Parliament

This fact, coupled with similar experiences gained by the other Communist and workers' parties, led to the possibility being envisaged of the transition of some countries from capitalism to socialism by revolutionary use of parliament. This road which was most clearly illuminated and generalized at the 20th Congress of the CPSU shows, at the present time, the real possibility of forming a government of broad democratic forces grouped round the workers' class, *relying on the revolutionary activity of the masses. Such a government can be set up without armed battle, by peaceful means.* Its installation would be practically tantamount to the establishment of the democratic revolutionary power of the people. (Therefore, about the same would be achieved, as was attained in our country, by the armed, bloody battle of the national and democratic revolution.) The purpose to which this new power, the nucleus of which would be formed by the workers' class, should be put thereafter would be the use of parliament for the consolidation and deepening of the real democratic rights and to a more or less speedy unfolding of the socialist revolution (Generally our tasks during the years 1945–1948). The use of parliament *itself* for the transfer of all power into the hands of the workers' class, the speed of progress and the order of its revolutionary tasks, would be, however, the same as the methods of the struggle — variegated — and would always correspond with the specific class and historical conditions.

Despite these differences there are in existence fundamental, generally valid conditions for the possibility of a revolutionary use of parliament on the road to socialism, the substance of which is revolutionary and which are to be clearly distinguished from the reformist conception of the aim and use of Parliament. Our own Czechoslovak experience has also contributed to the generalization and practical proof of the validity of these principles.

The most important of these lies in the necessity of combining the revolutionary activity of parliament with a systematic development and the organization of revolutionary actions on the part of broad popular masses.

The Combination of "Pressure From Above" and that "From Below" — One of the Elementary Conditions for the Revolutionary Use of Parliament.

A preliminary condition for carrying out fundamental social changes and for making it possible that parliament be made use of for the purpose of transforming a capitalist society into a socialist one, is: *(a) to fight for a firm parliamentary majority which would ensure and develop a strong pressure from "above," and (b) to see to it that this firm parliamentary majority should rely on the revolutionary activity of the broad working masses exerting pressure "from below."* The elementary condition for success consists, therefore, of a combination of pressure from "above" with that from "below" and its joint effect on the unfolding and strength of the revolution. This connection of the form of fighting from "above" with that from "below" emanates from the principle that questions regarding the class struggle (and, all the more, the social revolution) are decided and can be decided by strength alone. The pressure from "above" is a combination of preparations of the conditions for the creation and organization of the strength of the revolution, for its aggressiveness and its drive.

Pressure From Above

(a) Regarding Questions of Using Pressure from "Above"

The possibility and necessity of using tactical pressure from above in the stage of the democratic revolution was emphasized by the classics of Marxism-Leninism. In 1873, F. Engels criticized the Spanish nihilists (lit.: Bakuninists; Tr.) for not making use of pressure from above for the development of the democratic revolution. In 1905, V. I. Lenin proclaimed:

1. "To restrict, as a principle, revolutionary actions to pressure from below and to forgo pressure from above, is anarchism.
2. "Whoever cannot grasp the new tasks in the era of revolution, the tasks of actions, from above, whoever cannot state the conditions for and the program of such actions, that person has no idea of the tasks of the proletariat in any democratic revolution.
3. "*The principle that it is not admissible for social democracy (i.e., the revolutionary party of the proletariat) to take part, jointly with the bourgeoisie, in a provisional revolutionary government, that every such participation should rate as betrayal of the workers'*

class, is a principle of anarchism." (V. I. Lenin, "Spisy," Vol. 8, Czech edition 1954. p. 477.)

The Bolsheviks were to have participated in the envisaged provisional revolutionary government in the bourgeois democratic revolution in Russia in 1905, with this aim: to lead a heedless fight against all counter-revolutionary efforts and to protect the independent interests of the workers' class. *The overall character of the participation in this government was: not to lose from sight, even for a moment, the carrying out of a complete socialist coup.*

Suppressing the Counter-revolution

Pressure from "above" is, therefore, the pressure of a revolutionary government, parliament and the other organs of power in the state apparatus or its parts and it has, in substance, a dual effect — the direct suppression by power of the counter-revolution and its machinations and, at the same time, the exertion of pressure on the citizens, inciting and organizing them for the struggle for a further development of the revolution. A most important lesson for the whole of the international workers' movement (and by this for our Party as well) was learned from the experience gained during the era of the Popular Front in Spain and France. In particular, the example of Spain showed that as a result of the weakness of the Communists who did not stand at the head of the whole movement, the pressure from "above" was weakened. The Republican government, whose leading force was the Liberals, refused to meet the demands of the Communists who pressed for a purge of fascist generals from the army , so the army was preserved for the counter-revolution, the army which later became the main force of the victorious counter-revolutionary uprising.

Our workers' class and the CPCS gained valuable experience from the course of the struggle from "above" and the various forms of application in the new conditions. What were the principal forms of pressure "from above" applied in the period of the transformation of our national and democratic revolution into a socialist one?

Step One: Isolating the Bourgeoisie

The first direction given to the pressure "from above," which our workers' class applied from its position of power in the organs and newly forming links of the apparatus of the people's democratic state, was a systematic fight against enemies, traitors and collaborators. *Gradually, as the national and democratic revolution changed into a socialist one, the pressure "from above" was applied in an ever-increasing measure for the direct suppression and destruction of the counter-revolutionary machinations of the bourgeoisie.* Let us recall the signal role played in the development and extension of that pressure by the Ministry of the Interior, for instance, which was led by the Communists and the units of State Security directed by them.

But also other organs of the state and of the state apparatus controlled by the Communists also served for the direct suppression of bourgeois sabotage and obstructionism. So, for instance, the *Ministry of Agriculture* quickly completed, by means of so-called "roving commissions" (lit.: flying commissions; Tr.) the confiscation of the land of enemies and traitors, which had been sabotaged in the autumn of 1946 by the bourgeoisie. The national committees organized in autumn 1947 the "Special Food Commissions" which uncovered the hidden stores of landowners and kulaks and contributed greatly in this way to their isolation. In December 1947 organs of the Ministry of Internal Trade, controlled by the Communists uncovered an extensive black market in the textile trade organized by the bourgeoisie, and liquidated, for all practical purposes, the private capitalist textile wholesale business by the setting up of state textile distribution centers.

The organs holding powers and the components of the state controlled by Communists, in this way, became unusually effective levers for the defense of the revolutionary achievements of the people and for the further advancement of the revolution. They made it possible to suppress directly bourgeois counter-revolutionary elements (to render harmless their sabotage and subversion). They made an outstanding contribution to the isolation of the bourgeoisie. They gave impetus to the revolutionary determination and self-confidence of the working masses. And so they formed a mighty support and force furthering the revolution.

Step Two: Popularizing Revolutionary Demands

The second prong of the pressure "from above" successfully employed by our workers' class was the use made of the organs holding powers (the government, parliament, national committees) for bringing about a wide popularization of revolutionary demands and slogans. So, for instance, the government approved the "Program of Building" elaborated by the Communists, which, in its substance, was a program for the further transformation of the democratic revolution into a socialist one. Its passage was of immense importance since the program of the next economic-political measures for advancing the revolution, elaborated by the Communists, became the program of the entire government. This later enabled the workers' class to uncover all attempts made by the bourgeoisie at thwarting it as evidence of the anti-people, treacherous policy of the bourgeoisie and to isolate its political exponents. At the same time, because of the fact that revolutionary demands and recommendations were sponsored directly by organs of the state, they gave an unusually effective incentive for the revolutionary initiative of the masses. Examples of the far-reaching results in closing the ranks of the working masses round the slogans of the Party were, e.g., the proposal of the Communists in the government recommending the introduction of the Millionaires' Levy, the draft proposals of the Agricultural Laws elaborated by the Communist-controlled Ministry of Agriculture and submitted to the working peasants for comment, and other things. The fact that such demands and recommendations emanated directly from the highest state organs had a strong influence on their popularization and gave an exceptionally strong impetus to the revolutionary élan of the masses who pressed for their implementation. (So, e.g., the notice for the preliminary registration of all land exceeding 50 hectares, issued by the Ministry of Agriculture in the course of the struggle for the implementation of the third phase of the people's democratic land reform, had the effect of the working peasants in all villages realizing, when the registration was carried out, what land was beyond their reach and how much of it there was; of their visualizing the possibility of getting hold of it soon and, therefore, the effect of an increasingly more determined and decisive stand being taken in favor of carrying out the proposed reform.)

This direction given to the pressure "from above," therefore, served particularly the wide popularization of the demands and slogans of the policy of the Communists designed for a speedy progress of the revolution. It served as a means for the revolutionary education and organization of the popular masses.

Step Three: Nationalizing the Economy

A particularly important and exceptionally effective way of the struggle "from above" lay in the utilization of economic political power positions, especially the nationalization of the banks, of banking, of key and big industries.

The economic power positions of the workers' class, represented by the nationalized sector of the country's economy, were a mighty lever for the development of pressure "from above." It made possible the suppression and, to a considerable extent, the paralyzing of bourgeois counter-revolutionary intrigues aimed at economic decline and chaos. On the other hand, these positions also made possible the exerting of "pressure" on the citizens and broad masses of the working people. The fast expansion of nationalized production and the resulting rise in the standard of living of working people presented examples in point showing the advantages of a nationalized and, in its substance, working-class-controlled and -directed production; gave rise to revolutionary self-confidence and determination on the part of the working people and thus contributed to a still further isolation of the bourgeoisie.

This method of pressure "from above" was, therefore, a mighty pillar and force of the progressing (lit.: deepening; Tr.) revolution.

Step Four: Using Power to Silence Opposition

The fourth direction given to the pressure "from above" existed in the utilization of the organs holding power for the direct uncovering of the anti-people policy of the bourgeoisie, for the isolation of the reactionary bourgeois leadership of the other parties of the National Front.

All organs vested with powers (the national committees, Parliament, the government) became places for the workers' class in which the anti-people policy of the bourgeoisie and of its parties was being uncovered. The Communists made use of these organs for sharp criticism levelled against the other parties and their representatives on the grounds of inconsistency and obstructionism regarding the fulfillment of the tasks accepted in the program (in Parliament, for instance, the criticism and uncovering of the anti-people activity of the Ministry of Justice which was controlled by the National Socialist Party, the uncovering of the obstructionist inactivity of the Ministry of Food, controlled by the rightist Social Democrat Majer, etc.). At the same time, these organs holding power were used for tabling further demands and proposals in favor of the working people and, in this way, the bourgeoisie and its minions were forced either to their acceptance or to an open showing of their anti-people's face. (How important for the isolation of the bourgeois leadership of the other parties of the National Front was the proposal of the Millionaires' Levy alone, tabled in the government by the Communists in 1947 and at first rejected by its majority!)

These disclosures were especially tilted at those parties which professed to be socialist by their name and slogans, particularly at the National Socialist Party and the right wing of the Social Democratic Party. Their lying slogans and bourgeois conception of socialism were uncovered by the hand of their concrete activity within the organs, and their "socialist cloak" was torn from them before the eyes of the working people.

All the basic forms and actions involving pressure "from above" employed by our workers' class in the years 1945-1948 conformed, in the new circumstances, with the tasks allotted to the pressure "from above" as predicted by Lenin — a fight without quarter against all counter-revolutionary attempts and the defense of the independent interests of the working class. By using these methods this principle was fulfilled in practice: *not to lose sight for a single moment of the aim of a complete socialist overthrow.*

The individual forms and actions of the struggle "from above" carried out by our workers' class in the years 1945–1948 meant making use of the positions held by the workers' class in the organs vested with powers, and in the entire state and economic apparatus for strengthening the people's democratic power, for weakening and isolating the bourgeoisie, for conquering its positions by the workers' class and for the consolidation of the revolutionary democratic people's power in the dictatorship of the proletariat.

These forms and actions of the struggle "from above" — always serving the release, the mobilization and organization of the revolutionary forces of the popular masses — greatly enriched the tactical armament and experience of the international workers' movement.

Our practice and successes in the struggle "from above" made a trenchant contribution to the generalization of the experience gained and toward outlining the possibilities of a revolutionary use of parliament during the transition to socialism.

Pressure From Below

(b) Questions of Utilizing Pressure "From Below"

To bring about a parliament which would cease to be a "soft-soap factory" and would become a revolutionary assembly of working people requires, however, a force constituting, maintaining, and actively assisting its revolutionary activity. This force, necessary for breaking the resistance of the reactionary bourgeoisie, exists in the pressure by the popular masses "from below." Whereas pressure "from above" is the pressure exerted by the organs of the state and of the state apparatus for the direct suppression, by power, of the counter-revolution which helps, at the same time, to rally and organize the popular masses for the fight for further progress of the revolution, pressure "from below" is the pressure exerted by the popular masses on the government, on parliament and on other organs holding power. This pressure takes effect mainly in three directions:

(a) it systematically supports the revolutionaries in the organs of power, enhances their strength and *makes up for numerical weakness;*
(b) it has a direct effect on limiting the influence and positions of waverers and enemies standing in the path of the further progress of the revolution;
(c) it awakens the forces of the people dormant for many years, their energy and self-confidence; *it breaks through the onerous circle of intimidation and spiritual terror of the old institutions, the Church, etc.*

The pressure "from below," the revolutionary emergence of the popular masses, is, therefore, essential for the success of every revolution. In the February revolution in France in 1848 the provisional government, in which there were only two representatives of the workers, refused to declare the republic. However, it was forced to do so by the threat of the armed proletariat. The pressure "from below" prompted the provisional government to act. When, however, the Paris proletariat came out in unreserved support of the provisional government in the March demonstrations, it was defeated from the beginning.

> "It consolidated the position of the provisional government instead of subordinating it''
>
> — (K. Marx, "The Class Struggle in France." K. Marx–F. Engels, "Vybrane Spisy," I, page 156.)

When Lenin clarified the possibility of and conditions for the participation of the revolutionary workers' party in the provisional revolutionary government in 1905, at the height of the bourgeois democratic revolution in Russia, he sharply stressed: "We are obliged to influence the provisional revolutionary government from below in any event.'' (V. I Lenin, "Selected Writings," I, page 456.)

In 1936*, when the Seventh Congress of the Communist International elaborated the line of a united and popular front and the government possibilities of a united or popular front, the necessity of pressure brought to bear on such a government by the revolutionary masses was stressed:

> "Since this movement of a united front is a militant movement against fascism and the reactionaries, it will be a constant movable force driving the government of the united front into the fight against the reactionary bourgeoisie . . . And the better this mass movement is organized from below, the broader the network of supra-party class organs of the united front in the factories, among the unemployed in the labor districts, among the little men in towns and villages, the more guarantees will exist against a possible rejection of the policy of the government of the united front." (G. Dimitrov, "Digest from Speeches and Articles," 1950, page 103.)

*Should read "1935." Error in original.

Communist Party Prescription: "Pressure From Below"

The principle and the necessity of using pressure from below by the popular masses, forming one of the fundamental possibilities of making revolutionary use of parliament, as mentioned at the 20th Congress of the CPSU, ties in fully with the old practice of the revolutionary workers' classes in parliament also in the new conditions. Therefore, the revolutionary workers' movement must bring pressure to bear from below on parliament and the government whenever it wishes to protect, consolidate and extend the achievements of the revolution. It is in this pressure of the revolutionary masses, purposefully led by the revolutionary workers' party, that there exists a source of strength, power, courage and energy of the revolutionary Parliament, breaking the resistance of the reactionary forces; that there exists an instrument of the real will of the people which is capable of playing an exceptional part in the "peaceful'' transformation of the capitalist society into a socialist one. And it is this principle of utilizing purposeful development and organization of pressure "from below'' referred to at the 20th Congress of the CPSU, which stands out in the sharpest contrast with the old reformist theory and practice of the "Parliamentary road'' which isolates and forgoes the pressure of the popular masses.

Our workers' class and the CPCS gained valuable experience also from the waging of the fight "from below," and the various forms of its application. Of particular importance is the experience with the great variety of forms of directing the pressure "from below,'' guaranteeing for the CPCS the leadership of the workers' class and of the broad popular masses.

The very conception of the existing broad National Front

contributed to attaining this end. It consisted not only of the political parties but also broad united national mass organizations, the establishment of which the CPCS achieved with the help of the revolutionary activity of the masses. These organizations comprised broader masses than the political parties; they fortified the unity of the people and, at the same time, considerably reinforced the positions of the workers' class and the positions of left progressive democratic forces in the other parties of the National Front. The united mass organizations, which were led and influenced to a large extent by the Communists, represented, in this way, virtually the direct reserves of the Party. Through them the strong influence of the policy of the Communists also penetrated into the other political parties and thus the unity of the National Front was strengthened from below over the heads of the leaders.

Use of National Mass Organizations

Of quite exceptional importance was the origin of the United Revolutionary Trade Union Movement (ROH). ROH, as a class and socialist organization, consolidated the unity of the workers' class; it enhanced its revolutionary strength and weight and, under the leadership of the Communist Party, it used this strength most effectively for the fortification of the people's democratic power and for the advancement of the socialist revolution.

Other means for influencing and guiding the working masses were in particular: The United Association of Czech Peasantry, the Association of Liberated Political Prisoners, the Association of Friends of the Soviet Union, the C.S. Youth Federation, etc. A great help for the guidance and organization of the revolutionary fight of the peasants were the so-called "Peasants' Commissions," whose members could be only farmhands, tenant farmers and small and medium farmers from the ranks of applicants for land.

This network of broad national mass organizations was used by the Communists for the popularization of their policy and slogans, and for engendering and organizing the initiative of the masses and for using the various forms and actions of the pressure "from below" for the purpose of implementing that policy.

Use of Protests, Demonstrations, and Strikes

The second experience gained in the struggle "from below" is the many-sided use of the proper forms of pressure exerted by the popular masses. These forms corresponded to the complicated class situation in the conditions prevailing under the people's democratic order, when the workers' class assumed power but the bourgeoisie still kept part of the power. On the one side, all the old proven forms of the struggle of the popular masses were employed, the forms which were in keeping with the revolutionary initiative and determination of the workers and matched the degree of resistance shown by the bourgeoisie: *calling of protest meetings, passing of resolutions, sending of delegations, organizing mass demonstrations and also, eventually using strikes, including general strikes* (when finally the open political clash with the bourgeoisie was brought about in February 1948).

The strength and striking power of the individual actions of the pressure "from below" were constantly increased as need arose, and were safeguarded by exceptional organizational forms. An especially prominent role was played in this by the "Congresses of Factory Councils" and the "Congresses of Peasants' Commissions" (when the political crisis was resolved in Slovakia in the autumn of 1947; in the struggle for nationalization of private capitalist enterprises with over 50 employees and the entire domestic and foreign wholesale business; when the demand was pressed home for land reform above 50 hectares; and when the political crisis was settled in February 1948).

On the other side, the Communists, aided by the network of national mass organizations (and by the pressure "from above" exerted by the organs holding powers, especially the national committees and the government), developed new forms of pressure "from below," meeting the situation when the workers' class was proceeding with the assumption of power. These forms must be particularly noted. They are the organization of a broad building movement on the basis of voluntary brigades (coal, harvest, machine, etc.), and the advancement of competition in production within the factory and on a state-wide scale. These "constructive" forms of pressure "from below" fortified the overall position of the people's democratic state, paralyzed the efforts of the bourgeoisie to bring about an economic and political upheaval and, through their results (fast economic consolidation of the country and a rising standard of living of the working people), permanently entrenched and reinforced the power positions of the workers' class in the country.

This third most valuable experience gained by our workers' class is the creative application of the principal condition for pressure "from below," much emphasized by Lenin, that is to say *arming the proletariat.* (V. I. Lenin stressed, in his work "Two Tactics," two principal conditions for the pressure from below: the proletariat must be armed because the threat of a civil war exists, and the proletariat must be led by a revolutionary workers' Party.)

The workers' class armed itself in the course of the national and democratic revolution. Even after the victory of that revolution it retained its arms, however. One part of it, from the ranks of the partisans, barricade-fighters and from the units of the C.S. corps formed in the Soviet Union, became the nucleus of a new armed state apparatus, especially the security apparatus under the control of the Ministry of the Interior which was in the hands of the Communists.

The second part , the so-called Factory Guards, permanently secured the safety of the works. In case of danger of an attack by the counter-revolution, individual parts of the workers' class were armed: in the summer of 1947 the former partisans were armed for the liquidation of the Bender groups in Slovakia and, in February 1948, when the preparations for a counter-revolutionary conspiracy by the bourgeoisie were uncovered, strong, armed people's militias were formed. In the last instance, it was the arming of the workers' class which took away the bourgeoisie's liking for an armed conflict, which prevented bloodshed and ensured the undisturbed course of the revolution. (The necessity of arming the most mature part of the workers' class for repulsing the counter-revolutionary machinations of the bourgeoisie and for ensuring the undisturbed building of socialism has been proved, incidentally, again by the later formation of the workers' militias in people's democratic Hungary and Poland.)

The armed parts of the workers' class thus represented a very real and concrete form of the pressure "from below" directed against the counter-revolution and a very concrete and effective support for the workers' forces in the organs of the state.

Of great importance for the international workers' movement are not only the experience gained in the individual forms and actions of the pressure "from below" (corresponding to the concrete historical conditions), but also the absolute necessity of such a pressure as proved again by the actual practice which ended in victory. The pressure of the popular masses "from below" (in the totality of all its forms and concrete actions) made it impossible for the representatives of the other parties of the National Front, controlled by the bourgeoisie, which had numerical superiority in the decisive organs endowed with power, to isolate the Communists and to stop the revolution. Thus it (the pressure . . .; Tr.) made up for the numerical weakness of the revolutionary representatives of the workers' class in these organs and enhanced their strength; it contributed in a decisive manner to the acceptance of further revolutionary measures weakening the bourgeoisie and fortifying the power of the workers' class. *This experience, that pressure "from below" is absolutely essential for the undisturbed unfolding of the socialist revolution, is also reflected, in full measure in the theory about the possibility of the revolutionary utilization of parliament in connection with the road to socialism.*

The combination of the pressure "from above" with that "from below" — the path toward the progressive, undisturbed breaking of the resistance of the bourgeoisie, toward the gradual limitation and making impossible of a show of force by the bourgeoisie. *The real possibility of the revolutionary utilization of parliament for the road to socialism lies, therefore, in the combined mass strength of the revolutionary acting people supporting parliament as a revolutionarily active assembly which fights for the systematic fulfillment of the demands of the working people.* This coordination of actions by the broad popular masses and the revolutionary forces in parliament, in the government and in the local organs of power, mutually germinates their strength, drives the revolution ahead and infuses it with attacking and penetrating power.

The Decisive Force

Can this force really render impossible, or reduce to a minimum, however, armed violence on the part of the bourgeoisie? This question is very topical and it is discussed especially among the comrades of those Communist Parties who have orientated themselves toward a peaceful transition toward the socialist revolution. Let us take an example from France, where, after the 20th Congress of the CPSU, a controversy developed in the periodical *France Nouvelle* between comrades H. Iannucci and Florimont Bonte.

"When reading F. Bonte's article," Comrade Iannucci writes, "we gain the impression that the bourgeois state consists of parliament alone and not also of a powerful bureaucratic, military and police apparatus which has grown substantially under imperialism. In our social order great political problems are settled behind the scenes, the exchanges, or in administrative bodies rather than in parliament. . .

"Is it at all possible to imagine that in a country such as France, which has a strong and most dexterous bourgeoisie, which has a model administration and possesses, thanks to colonial wars and the suppression of internal disorders, strong armed and police forces — why, could one imagine that the bourgeoisie here would 'resign' because of a mere 'decree of parliament' or without 'civil war,' without an 'armed uprising'?" *(France Nouvelle,* 1956, No. 542.)

Comrade F. Bonte replied to the doubts expressed by Comrade Iannucci and attempted to disperse them, referring to Engels' idea that as soon as the workers' class gains the support of the masses, of the working peasantry and of other exploited sections, it will become "the decisive force, to which all the other forces will have to submit willy-nilly."

Let us try to imbue this theory with the life of our practice and to render it clearer and more convincing in this way. Let us first take, however, a concrete instance of how the pressure from "above" was combined with that "from below" in a situation in which Parliament was already playing a powerful role in our development.

Confiscation of Private Land

In accordance with the Kosice government program, the first big transfer of land was effected in people's democratic Czechoslovakia. 2,946,395 ha [hectares] of land belonging to big holders, enemies and traitors was confiscated and allotted, on the basis of decrees, to 305,148 families of agricultural workers, tenants and small-holders, and put partly under the administration of the co-operatives, national committees and the state. This land reform resulted in the almost complete liquidation of big holdings of land in the border regions, but the central parts of the country were affected by these decrees to only an insignificant measure. Big landowners, holding above 50 ha of land, and the Church still retained some 1,400,000 ha of agricultural land, which means almost a fifth of the entire land. An economically and numerically strong section of kulaks still represented a very important force of the bourgeoisie in the countryside and the bourgeoisie was still most influential with the medium farmers as well.

The possibility of a further successful advance of the revolution depended on the reinforcement of the influence of the workers' class and of the CPCS in the countryside, on a further strengthening and widening of the bond between the workers' class and the working peasantry. The road for this was the struggle for further demands of the peasants (especially the still unquenched thirst for land), a more intensive campaign for uncovering the face of the bourgeoisie and further subversion of the biggest bastion of the bourgeoisie in the countryside — the landholders' ownership of the land.

In the summer of 1946, the Communists began the fight for

handing over more land to the working peasantry (simultaneously with the demands that the allotted land should be speedily registered in the land rolls, that hunting rights should be democratized, boundary adjustments should be effected and the splitting up of agricultural land should be prevented and that the agricultural production plan should be safeguarded). They demanded a revision of the land reform of 1919, which the bourgeoisie had carried out in the pre-Munich republic. The revision affected a total of 1,027,529 ha of land and its materialization would mean the complete liquidation of the group of big landowners with over 150 ha of arable or 250 ha of agricultural land, the group of the so-called "rest-estate holders" and land speculators.

The demand for the revision of the first land reform of 1919 was pressed home by the Communists in the program of the new government after the elections in May 1946 ("The Building Program"). In the autumn of 1946 the Ministry of Agriculture, controlled by the Communists, submitted this demand (along with others) as a draft bill to the working peasantry for their comments (the so-called six Duris Acts). The fight proper for carrying out a revision of the first land reform was, therefore, started by pressure from above.

The acceptance of the demand for a revision was bound to affect severely the big land-owners and the countryside bourgeoisie and, by this, the bourgeoisie as a whole. The bourgeoisie, making use of its positions in the leadership of the other parties of the National Front, in Parliament and in the government, therefore, started to put up resistance against it immediately. It tried to prevent the acceptance of this law or to clip it and, in this way, to retain big land-ownership. A sharp class fight with the bourgeoisie developed over the acceptance of this law.

Pressure From Above Triggers Pressure From Below

The pressure "from above" exerted by the Ministry of Agriculture (i.e., emanating directly from the supreme organ of the state — the government) by coming out with the draft law and openly inviting thc working peasantry to comment on and to support it, triggered off, at the same time, a strong pressure "from below."

The peasants discussed the draft proposals of the law at their meetings and their overwhelming majority demanded its acceptance. In the villages in which there was land subject to revision, "Peasants' Commissions" were set up as the organs of the landless, small and medium farmers — applicants for land. The demand for the revision was backed up more and more strongly by the local national committees (representing pressure from below, vis-à-vis the higher administrative organs, Parliament, and the leadership of the other parties of the National Front), by the United Association of Czech Peasantry and by the local organizations of the other political parties.

Liquidation of Private Property

To increase the effectiveness of the pressure "from above" and "from below" against the bourgeoisie, the Communists proclaimed (on behalf of the Ministry of Agriculture) additional far-reaching demands for the working peasantry, the so-called "Hradec Program." Its basic demand was the division into lots of all big estates of over 50 ha and the complete liquidation of land held for the purpose of investment [lit.: speculation; Tr.] (Furthermore the introduction of peasants' insurance, grants of agricultural credits and protection to peasants, the introduction of a uniform agricultural tax graded in accordance with production areas, the size of farms, the number of dependents, etc., a speedy mechanization of agriculture aided by the state, especially the establishment of State Tractor and Machine Stations).

The area of land subject to division according to this demand amounted to 432,905 ha, situated in 9,540 parishes, i.e., in two thirds of all the parishes in the whole state. This meant that additional masses of small and medium farmers were drawn into the decisive fight for the liquidation of big estate ownership (and the other demands). The struggle for the revision of the first land reform entered the next, decisive stage. In the summer the proposal of the law was debated by *Parliament.* The Communists used these debates for uncovering the bourgeois leadership of the National Socialist, the Popular and the Democratic parties, and proved them to be furious defenders of the land owners and enemies of the working peasantry. Every attempt of the bourgeoisie at thwarting, delaying or limiting the proposed law was brought out into the open by the Communists in Parliament and pilloried. On June 9 and 10 alone the central organ of the Party, "Rude Pravo," published a number of such disclosures made on the floor of *Parliament* ("The Representatives of the Big Land-Owners in *Parliament* Against the Peasants," "They Wanted to Give the Big Land-Owners and Rest-Estate Holders Millions of Hectares of Forestry Land," "The Secretary General of the National Socialist Party, Dr. Krajina, Threw the Peasants out of the Lobby of National Socialist National Assembly Members," etc.).

The Communist pressure in the government and in *Parliament* (the pressure "from above") engendered more and more decisively the pressure "from below." Thousands of resolutions from meetings of peasants demanding the immediate acceptance of these laws were submitted to Parliament and the government. The resolutions, which were also signed by the village organizations of the National Socialist, Popular and Democratic parties, said: "...we now recognize who is with us and who is against us." Dozens of Peasants' Commissions, composed of members of all the political parties, came to Parliament and stormily warned the leadership of the bourgeois parties not to obstruct their demands, claiming their immediate implementation. (For instance, the largest of these delegations was composed of 57 members of the National Socialist party, 35 members of the Popular party, 38 Social Democrats, 153 Communists, 15 members without political allegiance, and 48 members who did not state to which party they belonged.)

On July 11, the pressure from "above" and from "below" closed like the claws of a pair of pincers. The bourgeoisie, whose political positions were perceptibly shaken, had to give way. The bill on revision of the first agricultural reform was passed by the Parliament. The consequences of this victory were: the liquidation of more of the economic positions of the bourgeoisie in the village, a big political defeat of the bourgeoisie (its increasing isolation), a considerable strengthening and broadening of the bond between the workers' class and the working peasantry. The peasants recognized that, given direct political, organizational and material help of the workers' class, they could lead a successful fight against their arch-enemy, the landowner and his helpers. Increasingly wider masses of peasants were coming over to Party positions and supported its political line aiming at further deepening of the revolution.

Industry Nationalized

By a similar method, the claws of the pincers were being closed by pressure from "above" and from "below" in the years 1945-1948, penetrating deeper and deeper into the flesh of the bourgeoisie. Thus, when the liquidation of the political and economic positions of the occupiers and of the treacherous native grand-bourgeoisie was completed in the course of the national and democratic revolution on the basis of the Kosice program, further groups of the bourgeoisie were gradually annihilated as the revolution progressed. The nationalization in October 1945 liquidated particularly the economic power of the financial bourgeoisie, the group of industrialists dominating until then the key industries and the basic sources of raw material and the group of factory owners employing over 500 employees.

Apart from the 62 per cent of the industry already nationalized another 13 per cent of the "small confiscates" were torn from the hands of private enterprises in spring of 1947. The revision of the first land reform signified the liquidation of the group of big landowners owning over 150 hectares of arable or 250 hectares of agricultural land, and the liquidation of the owners of "residue'' farms. In the autumn of 1947 these "pincers" helped to carry out the "Millionaires' Levy" and to solve the political crisis in Slovakia caused by the sabotage and counter-revolutionary activity of the strongest Slovak political party, the democrats.

All these class clashes with the bourgeoisie had far-reaching political consequences. The influence and strength of the bourgeoisie was collapsing; the broad masses gathered with growing resolution around the CPCS and its policy.

Undermining Political Opposition

At the end of 1947 and the beginning of 1948 an actual disintegration of the National Socialist, the People's and the Democratic parties, took place. Honest members of these parties were parting with their bourgeois leadership and were coming over to the ranks of the CPCS and the Slovak CP (by November 1947, when the Communists had gained 237,384 new members since the beginning of the year, the CPCS was stronger than all other political parties taken together), or created opposition groups within their own parties. The isolation of the bourgeoisie within the parties of the National Front was proceeding not only from thc outside, through the turning away of the broad masses from parties ruled by the bourgeoisie, but also from within, through the growth of democratic and socialist forces in these parties; through the growth of progressive opposition, seeking the maintenance and strengthening of people's democratic freedoms and rights and, therefore, endeavoring to cooperate with the Communists. From the bottom and over the heads of reactionary leaders of the other political parties the National Front grew constantly stronger as a class and social unity of the working people, recognizing the CPCS as its leader, the Party which worked toward a total socialist reconstruction of the country.

The progress of the class struggles confirmed that the CPCS would gain in the forthcoming elections a decisive majority and would achieve the fulfillment of its other demands with the help of a democratically manifested will of the people. It demanded the liquidation of all private capitalist enterprises employing over 50 people, a total liquidation of the group of local and foreign merchants and a total liquidation of landowners owning over 50 hectares of land.

Thus, the situation of the bourgeoisie was, at the beginning of 1948 on the eve of the new parliamentary elections, substantially different from that in 1946. While prior to the elections in 1946 the bourgeoisie had a relatively strong mass basis, the short time of less than two years of people's democratic development had been sufficient for the disintegration of the political army upon which it could formerly count. The broad masses of the people, especially working peasants, lost their illusions as regards the bourgeoisie and went over to the side of the workers' class in order to place the bourgeoisie and its anti-popular and treacherous policy into the right light in the eyes of our nations. In 1948, when the decisive fight between the workers' class and the bourgeoisie drew closer, the bourgeoisie had only a shade of the power and influence that it used to have in 1945. In this situation, the bourgeoisie, frightened by this peaceful progress of the revolution which kept removing and destroying its economic and political positions one after another and which threatened their complete annihilation within a short time, decided to violate the lawful ways and to achieve its counter-revolutionary aims through a coup. It was signaled by a government crisis provoked by the resignation of 12 ministers. But by this the bourgeoisie only offered another new and open evidence of its spirit of disruption; it achieved its own isolation and complete defeat. After five days of government crisis, the people settled their accounts with bourgeoisie reaction, legally and constitutionally (under consistent use of all forms of pressure from "above" and from "below").

The Revolution Consolidates Political Power

The representatives of the bourgeoisie and their agents were replaced in the government, absolutely legally and in accordance with the constitution valid since pre-Munich days (1920), by new representatives faithful to the people, selected from the ranks of the reconstituted National Front and recognizing the leading role of the Communists in the state; the government was nominated by the President of the Republic and was unanimously approved by *Parliament.*

As evidence of the fact that this form of transition of political power into the hands of the workers class was absolutely legal and constitutional (and this point has an extraordinary political importance), we shall use a spontaneous and very valuable opinion of an important bourgeois émigré, the former chief of the office of the President of the Republic, Jaromir Smutny:

"In their calculation they (i.e., the representatives of the bourgeois parties who submitted their resignation — J. K.) failed to take into consideration other fundamental circumstances:

"(a) that the government is not 'ipso facto' dissolved if a minority of its members resigns (according to the constitution, the government was able to pass decisions if more than half of its members were present, not counting the premier. In the case of the February government, 13 members made up an absolute majority);

"(b) that the premier could not be forced into resignation with the rest of his ministers unless given a vote of non-confidence by *the Parliament;*

"(c) that the President of the Republic had no constitutional right to make the premier resign when only part of his ministers left the government, even if the character of the government was substantially changed;

"(d) that only the national assembly had the power to force Gottwald to resign."

Yes."The irony of world history puts everything upside down. With us 'revolutionaries' and 'rebels' legal methods agree much more than illegal ones or than a coup. The parties of order, as they call themselves, die by the legal state which they created." (F. Engels, foreword to Marx' work "Class struggles in France," K. Marx — F. Engels: Selected Works, volume 1, 1950, p. 133)

And now let us return to the fears of Comrade Iannucci. Quite rightly, he draws attention to the fact that a bourgeois state is not just *theParliament* but also an enormous bureaucratic, military and police apparatus, and he asks in the light of this warning: "Is it possible to believe that the bourgeoisie would 'yield' by a simple 'act of parliament' or without a 'civil war,' without an 'armed uprising'?"

No, the bourgeoisie has never yielded its power by a simple "act of parliament." But it may be deprived of its power at an opportune moment without an armed uprising and civil war — by the force of consistently acting revolutionary masses led by the revolutionary workers' party, supporting their representatives in the parliament and transforming the parliament into an active revolutionary assembly.

In the fight for the direct national, democratic, peaceful, economic and social demands of the people, by a combined pressure from "above" and from "below," the position of the bourgeoisie in the organs of power and in the state apparatus may be weakened, step by step, and so may its economic positions, and thus the workers class heading the popular masses may be given, step by step, conditions more favorable for its fight for socialism. (Naturally, these demands will always be founded upon the concrete situation prevailing in the country concerned and will greatly differ. For example, defense of national interests by cancellation of all agreements and treaties with the United States of America damaging to the interests of the nation; prohibition of all war propaganda, punishment of warmongers and active support of the policy of collective security; abolition of all forms of racial, religious and national discrimination; fight against the monopolies, and their nationalization; carrying out of a land reform; introduction of a general system of social security; abolition of every kind of economic, social and legal inequality of women; separation of Church and state; etc.) In the course of the fight for these national, social, economic and political demands of broad masses of the working people, the following may and must be carried out successfully: a broadly founded democratization and reorganization of the organs of power (for instance, the principle that all the organs of state power, from top to bottom, are elected by the people; *the abolition of the senate and concentration of all power in the hands of the parliament;* a democratization and reorganization of the state apparatus — courts, police, army, etc.). This broad democratization is carried out, in principle, by the gradual destruction of the bourgeois state apparatus and its transformation into an instrument and source of power of the new democratic might. Therefore, the Eighth Congress of the Italian Communist Party, which worked out the Italian line to be taken on the road to socialism, emphasized that the parliament may and must carry out its active function, both in the interest of a democratic and socialist transformation of the country and in the new socialist society:

"It must be stated that the fundamental condition for its fulfilling this function is that it must take its initiative, impulses and inspiration for its regenerative activity from the new political and administrative system in the state — towns, provinces and regions — as defined by the constitution and the forms of directing democracy which are materialized through the participation of the workers' classes in the political-economic direction of the state." (Political resolution of the Eighth Congress of the Italian Communist Party, "Information Bulletin, International Political Questions," No. 1-2, p. 87.)

All these measures and their consequences (a systematic strengthening of the positions of power of the workers' class and the gradual weakening and destruction of the economic-political supports of the bourgeoisie) are, in their entirety, the actual way toward a limitation and perhaps exclusion of any violence of the bourgeoisie against the people and thus toward prevention of civil war. In this case, in the course of the fight for a complete takeover of all power by the workers' class, no notice can be taken of the present relationship between class forces; it must be considered what this relationship will be during the time of government of the revolutionary democratic might. Thus, at the moment when the bourgeoisie is in danger that all power is about to be taken over by the workers' class, it will be by far not so powerful and its main supports will be undermined.

Progress toward socialism may take, under these circumstances, a democratic and constitutional course. The parliament, which will be an active revolutionary assembly relying upon the revolutionary mass movement of the workers' class and its allies, will turn into an instrument of the workers' class on its way to power, into an instrument of the transformation of the whole state and its machinery. Under these circumstances, all the changes which, in their entirety, represent a revolutionary transformation of capitalist society into a socialist one will proceed absolutely legally. The parliament may pass, in a democratic and legal way and in the name of the nation, a new constitution codifying and making possible a socialist transformation of the country. (Within less than three months following the crushing of an attempted bourgeoisie coup, the Parliament of the Czechoslovak Republic approved a new constitution which safeguarded all the progress so far made and ensured the sovereignty of the working people in the state the popularization of the state apparatus and the liquidation of the remnants of the bureaucratic police state apparatus; anchored nationalization as a firm economic basis of the people's democratic state and, in its totality, strengthened and ensured the transition of the country to socialism.)

Thus, progress toward socialism, with the help of the parliament and without a bloody civil war, is a real possibility. However, this possibility must not raise false illusions among the workers' class which must not be, in the least, morally disarmed by doubts as to its right to take to arms in every case when forced to do so by the resistance of the bourgeoisie. Therefore, the 20th Congress of the Soviet Communist Party proclaimed with absolute frankness: *"There can be no doubt that for a number of capitalist countries a violent downthrow of the bourgeois dictatorship and, with it, a connected vehement acceleration of the class struggle is inevitable."*

Thus, the 20th Congress of the Soviet CP proclaims, in full harmony with the spirit of Marxism-Leninism, that at the present historical stage in the development of society, the possibility, of breaking the resistance of the bourgeoisie against socialist transformation of the society by non-violent means, without recourse to revolutionary violence, has matured or will mature in many countries. But the workers' class and working people will not renounce armed fight and revolutionary violence where it is inevitable in order to break the resistance of the exploiting classes. Thus, it uses Lenin's paraphrase: "A delivery may be difficult or easy. Naturally, we are all for an easy and painless delivery. Conditions for such a delivery are now favorable. But if necessary we are ready to undergo a difficult and painful delivery to see the child born."

Parliament: "A new instrument of socialist revolution"

Conflict between the revolutionary use of parliament and the reformist meaning of a "parliamentary way to socialism"

A revolutionary usefulness of the parliament will demand in new historical conditions, a realization of a new form of transition to the dictatorship of the proletariat; parliament must become a new instrument of socialist revolution depriving the bourgeoisie of its power, of its means of production and materializing the building of socialism with the working class directing the policy making. Thus, it serves the revolutionary aims of the proletariat and corresponds to the Marxist-Leninist principles of a necessity of revolutionary transition of the capitalist society into a socialist one, corresponds to Lenin's conclusions: " . . . capitalism cannot collapse but through a revolution." (V. I. Lenin: "Works," vol. 29 of Czech edition 1955, p. 394.) " . . . There can be no successful revolution without a suppression of the resistance of the exploiters." (V. I. Lenin: "Works," vol. 28 of Czech edition 1954, p. 66.) The reformist "parliamentary way to socialism" denies the necessity of a revolutionary transition of capitalist to socialist society, denies the necessity of a socialist revolution, denies the necessity (under the slogan of "parliamentary democracy") of seizure of all power by the workers' class, denies the necessity of acquiring the political direction of the state and of establishing the dictatorship of the proletariat. The reformist "parliamentary way" cannot, therefore, in its consequences, ever lead to the building up of socialism; is not, in its substance, a socialist program. It is capable of attacking within the framework of capitalism, with varying force, the consequences of capitalist exploitation but is not capable of grasping its causes, of smashing capitalism and materializing a revolutionary transformation of society.

These deep-rooted dissimilarities of the two approaches correspond to a similarly profound difference in the tactic in making use of the parliament.

The substance of the tactic of revolutionary use of the parliament is fully based upon the old principle of revolutionary activity of the workers class in a bourgeois parliament, worked out in detail by the classics of Marxism-Leninism and further developed in the new conditions. It starts from the following principle: Parliament in bourgeois countries is a product of historical development and cannot be erased from life. It is necessary, therefore, to work in it and to use it in the fight against bourgeois society.

The task of the representatives of the workers' class in the bourgeois parliament has always been to transform the parliament into a mirror showing the working masses the class interests and conflicts of bourgeois society in their nakedness and to unveil, consistently and unflinchingly, the bourgeoisie and its helpers (whether they are aware of their position or not). Their task has always been to use bourgeois parliament as a platform for revolutionary agitation, propaganda, and organization, as an effective form to unchain revolutionary activity of the broad popular masses, side by side with the workers' class.

Linking and systematic combination of parliamentary and non-parliamentary actions has always been the fundamental principle of revolutionary tactics in making use of the parliament.

This tactic of linking and combining of the parliament with revolutionary actions of the proletariat and the working masses outside the parliament, still used by Marxist-Leninist parties, may be given a new task in the new historical conditions and under the new circumstances; namely, to transform the parliament from an organ of the bourgeoisie into an instrument of power of the workers' class, and parliamentary democracy into an instrument for the establishment of a proletarian democracy, of a dictatorship of the proletariat.

The tactic of using parliament as a potential new specific form of transition to socialism is therefore only a further development, another step of the old Marxist-Leninist tactic combining the use of parliament with the use of the revolutionary masses, and is by its whole substance a complete antithesis to the reformist parliamentary way to socialism. In the same way as the revolutionary tactic of making use of the parliament corresponds to the revolutionary aims of the Marxist-Leninist party, the tactic of reformist use of parliament corresponds to the reformist aims of rejection of revolution.

To the reformists, parliament (an instrument of the bourgeoisie for strengthening and maintaining capitalist power) is an organ for cooperation between the workers' class and the bourgeoisie. Partial reforms achieved in the parliament (in agreement with the capitalists) serve the reformists as evidence that peaceful coexistence of bourgeoisie and the workers' class is possible, that class struggle is dying down, that revolution is superfluous and political domination of the workers' class unnecessary. Instead of the necessity of a proletarian democracy, they sustain the illusion of a parliamentary, pure democracy.

Because, in the reformist conception, parliament is an organ of cooperation of the workers' class with the bourgeoisie, the reformist tactic takes the weight of political work exclusively to the parliament (i.e., organ of bourgeois power), rejects and refuses the use of the pressure of broad popular masses, isolates parliament from the revolutionary actions of the working people. The reformists have already taken care, by their own deeds, of offering not one but scores of examples of the absolute impossibility and absurdity of their "parliamentary way to socialism."

The Socialist "Labour" Parties

In many countries the reformists won the majority, often absolute majority. Their governments were in existence, and have been in existence, for extended periods of time. One of the chief propagandists of this way, the British Labour Party, already has three times had an opportunity to turn its "theories" into practice. It held the government in 1924, in the years 1929 through 1931, and for six years in 1945 through 1951. The Swedish Social Democratic Party has for 25 years already, a whole quarter of a century, been the strongest and the governing party in the country (in this year's* elections to the Riksdag, the lower chamber of the Swedish parliament, it won 108 mandates, while the second strongest party, the Agrarian Union, obtained only 20 mandates). A similar situation prevails in other Nordic states. And still socialism is not built in these countries. To the contrary, capitalist domination grows stronger, the profits of the monopolies are rising.

There could be no clearer evidence of the absurdity of the idea that socialism may be built in cooperation with capitalism, without bringing down the political might of the bourgeoisie, without the dictatorship of the proletariat. (As a matter of fact, the bourgeoisie in capitalist states has a justified confidence in the reformists, as the present situation in France shows) While it breaks in one place, by a strike or by bloodshed and force of arms, it entrusts the "government" to the reformist socialists without hesitation if need be. And it knows why. A consistently conducted fight of the workers' class in

*1956

one single factory is more dangerous to it than a formal "entrusting with the government" to their helpers. In spite of its absolute hopelessness the theory of "a parliamentary way to socialism" is still alive in the capitalist states and appeals to the backward part of the working class and especially to the petty bourgeoisie (in view of the long, opportunistic influence exerted upon the masses which again is in direct connection with the idealization of parliamentarianism carried out by every means by the bourgeoisie).

Opportunist ideology and practice are, therefore, a serious obstacle to the creation of a broad and revolutionary movement of the masses fighting consistently for democratic and socialist demands. They are a serious obstacle to the efforts of the workers' class to transform the *parliament* into an instrument of power of the working class and must, therefore, be systematically and energetically fought.

The Communists and the workers' parties seeking to make a revolutionary use of the parliament in the fight for the transition to socialism may follow our advice from the time of the transition of the democratic revolution into a socialist revolution. This advice clearly demonstrates the grave danger of reformism and some of its concrete signs, which can be discovered even in the activity of the Social Democratic Party in conditions of the people's democratic system, a party which used to have a comparatively strong left leadership and followed a policy of cooperation with the Communists.

Accelerating the Communist Revolution

In the complicated class conditions of the years 1945-1948, when the question of power in people's democratic Czechoslovakia was not yet definitely settled and when power was still shared by the workers' party and the bourgeoisie, two basic political lines were opposing each other. One was the revolutionary political line of the workers' class, which had as its purpose and aim the achievement of a gradual isolation of the bourgeoisie and the closing of the ranks of the nation around the workers' class and its vanguard, the Communist Party. Its aim was the transition from the tasks of national and democratic revolution to the tasks of a socialist revolution and the definite settlement of the question of power by consolidating people's democracy into a state of the dictatorship of the proletariat. The second basic political line was the line of the bourgeoisie whose aim was to isolate the workers' class and its vanguard, the CPCS, to halt the national and democratic revolution and to attain with the help of Western imperialists the restoration of the capitalist domination under a dictatorship of the bourgeoisie.

In this tug-of-war situation, when the class struggle was accelerating, the workers' class fighting for complete political power was attacked from the rear by the reformist ideology and practice of the "democratic way to socialism" as preached by the right wing of the Social Democratic Party. While the workers' class under the leadership of the Communists was locked in battle with the bourgeoisie for a deeper and broader hegemony among all classes of working people, a battle for the strengthening and consolidation of its leading role in the nation, the reformists came forward with their theories denying the leading role of the proletariat and proclaiming its merging with (and thus absorption by) the other classes, for instance, with the peasantry.

The progress in agricultural production and the technical revolution in agriculture signify "that the peasantry moves with increasing momentum to the level of the workers, that the two massive sections of the working people become economically balanced and that thus the centuries-old wall between the worker and the peasant, between town and country, is inevitably disappearing. No doubt, this results in all the political consequences, for now the peasants as well become the bearers of technical and social, and thus also political (!) and cultural progress; like the workers, they uphold the struggle for a new social order (!) and take their place by the side of the workers in the socialist movement . . ." ("Minutes of the 20th congress of the Central Committee of the Social Democratic Party," page 80.)

This is a clear example of revision of the Marxist theory of classes. The peasantry (including the rich peasants who were the chief bearers of technical progress in our villages), the private owners of land, become, through the progress made in agricultural production (capitalist production) and through the introduction of technical means (as well as capitalist), just like the workers' class, the bearers of the struggle for the socialist social order. What else could the bourgeoisie wish, concentrating its efforts at breaking the hegemony of the workers' class in the nation? How far was this theory suppressing the difference in purpose of the individual classes and social groups in the socialist revolution from the voices of the bourgeoisie itself: "The nation is not composed of one occupation or class and it is to its benefit that all occupational and class interests be harmonized, for an excessive elevation or attenuation of one class must necessarily mark a detriment for the other classes and thus for the whole whose gain must be our only aim." ("Lidova Demokracie," 10.6.45.)

The "Democratic Way to Socialism"

It is as if this transparent wishful thinking were the father of the theory of a permanent peaceful coexistence of capitalism and socialism in one state, of the merging of antagonistic classes. "To us, nationalization or socialization of key positions in production and distribution and protection of private ownership of small and medium production units, and especially of private ownership of small and medium agricultural property, are an expression of a wise and economical organization. . . The materialization of this plan will lead to gradual elimination of class conflict in human society." ("Draft proclamation ...," page 566.)

Within the framework of this "democratic way to socialism," obstinately supported by the right wing of the Social Democratic Party, the private capitalist production sector was to be preserved permanently and so was the bourgeoisie with its still powerful economic foundation. Also permanently to be preserved was its position of strength, used to the dissipation of the country's economy and for political discrimination against the workers' class heading the state.

Also, the old reformist understanding of the role of *parliament* manifested itself under the influence of the right wing of social democracy, both in theory and practice, in the years 1945-1948 and was in crass conflict with the revolutionary line of using the parliament followed by the Communists. In complete accord with that line, the 20th Congress of the Social Democratic Party proclaimed that "the center of all political life will be the National Assembly" (p. 66). The proclamation of this principle was not made by chance. "In every (!) democracy parliament support for the will of the people is the most important." ("Social Democracy and the Rights of the National Assembly," "Cil," 1946, page 5.) "In the parliamentary system (bourgeois as well?) decisions are made before the eyes and under the direct control of the people." (V. Erban, "Svet Prace," 14.9.46)

What this meant in practice was well defined in A. Samek's article entitled "On the Reactionary Role of the Social Democratic Ideology of Transition of National and Democratic Revolution into a Socialist Revolution"

("Filosoficky Casopis," vol. 1955, No. l.):

"In practice this meant that whenever the people manifested its will otherwise than through its representatives in the National Assembly, the right wing of Social Democracy raised its voice in opposition to it. When in the course of the fight for the 'Hradec Program' the Communists appealed straight to the people and when the peasants approved this program at their meetings and sent their representatives to the National Assembly to voice their demands, the right wing of the Social Democratic Party reacted as follows: 'The Communists began to arrange public meetings of the peasants. This grew into a whole campaign organized with a view to compelling the National Assembly, also with the help of deputations dispatched to the parliament to pass the draft submitted by the Ministry of Agriculture without change. *With such influencing of the parliament and with these methods employed by the Minister, we could naturally not agree.'* (Report on activity, p. 13.) The people must not take a resolute position against the bourgeoisie; it is only allowed to discuss through its representatives in the *parliament*! When the bourgeoisie kept pronouncing, due to its position in the Ministry of Justice and in the Courts, disgracefully mild sentences against traitors and when the people raised their voices resolutely against this state of affairs, the CS Social Democratic press wrote that the Courts (in the given case, the bourgeoisie), and not the street (i.e., the working people), should judge. When the SNB takes steps against the enemies of people's democracy, when it openly defends the interests of the people and not those of the bourgeoisie, the Report complains as

> to the 'political influencing and misusing of the security apparatus' (p. 48). When the National Assembly discusses the bill on the enlightenment of officers of the security force, CS Social Democratic deputies submit a resolution stating that political education of the SNB is unnecessary! Thus the workers' class was to be deprived of its important weapon. On 2 July, 1946, 'Pravo Lidu' writes that CS Social Democracy will not let itself be influenced by public proclamations, stoppages of work, demonstrations, etc. These facts prove clearly that Social Democracy opposes the true rule of the people and tries to undermine the political activity of the working people, limit their political horizon, and make them a helpless tool in the hands of bourgeois politicians."

This characteristic may be supplemented by an example demonstrating how the theory and practice of Social Democratic isolation of parliament from the revolutionary struggle of the masses of working people suited the bourgeoisie. When, in the fall of 1945, the bourgeoisie opposed the decree nationalizing key and heavy industries, the CPCS decided to appeal to the people. A gigantic mass movement for nationalization ensued, pressing the bourgeoisie with its back against the wall. The bourgeoisie, afraid of the pressure of the popular masses, proclaimed: "We consider any pressure demanding an accelerated approval of the decree to be harmful. The government needs nothing more than peace and time . . . ." ("Lidova Demokracie," 26.9.45.)

The pressure of the people's masses holding the bourgeoisie in its pincers was to be relaxed. The Social Democratic Minister of Industry, Lausman, attempted at the decisive moment to frustrate the political activity of the working people. "Folks, have patience, the draft decree on nationalization of big industry has 46 paragraphs and we are arguing the first." ("Pravo Lidu," 24.9.45)

From Capitalism to Socialism Through Democracy

In order that the reformist "democratic way" to socialism be complete, there had to be, of course, a denial of the basic condition of the possibility of victory for socialism — of the dictatorship of the proletariat. "Our state has decided for socialization in the democratic manner, that is to say, through the ballot and not through revolution and dictatorship." ("Minutes of the 20th congress of the Social Democratic Party," page 161.) Thus, solving the problems of transition from capitalism to socialism, of breaking the desperate resistance of the bourgeoisie, of expropriating the exploiters and transforming small private capitalist production into socialist production on a large scale, should be possible without the direction of policy by the workers' class, without the dictatorship of the proletariat — just by phrases about some kind of pure democracy; in other words, revision and denial of the basic maxim of Marxist-Leninist theory of classes and class struggle.

The reformist theory and practice of the "parliamentary way," although flavored by new conditions, remained what it has always been, even on the soil of people's democracy, a theory and practice of the defense of the bourgeoisie. Its aim was the undermining of the leading role of the working class in the revolution, for it denied the necessity itself of a revolution, proclaimed the possibility of a permanent cooperation with the bourgeoisie, attempted to isolate Parliament from the revolutionary pressure of the working people and preserve it as an organ for co-operation with the bourgeoisie, negated the necessity of a dictatorship of the proletariat, and instead of a necessity of a proletarian democracy it nurtured illusions of "pure democracy." Therefore even in the people's democratic system in which the working people under the leadership of the Communist Party are able to see daily, in the course of attaining political, economic and social demands, the result of their revolutionary unity and of the perfidy of the reactionary bourgeoisie, it was necessary to fight systematically against the destructiveness of reformism subservient to the bourgeoisie. The Social Democratic Party, which, as a whole, was already following the policy of cooperation with the Communists, was purposely cited as an example of the strong influence of reformism and of its dangers. Much more open and also much more transparent was the reformism of the National Socialist Party proclaiming "national socialism," definitely rejecting Marx' theory and attempting, without shame, to strengthen capitalism. This warning experience convincingly points to one of the basic conditions of a revolutionary use of Parliament for the purpose of transition to socialism; namely, to the necessity of "decisive rejection of opportunist elements unable to drop the policy of compromise with the capitalists and landowners." (20th congress of the Soviet CP, "Nova Mysl," February 1956, p. 23.)

Therefore, if the workers' class is to create under its leadership a united revolutionary popular movement able to break the resistance of the reactionary bourgeois forces, if it is to transform a bourgeois parliament into an organ of the will of the working people and to use it as an instrument for a peaceful transition to socialism, it must fight systematically and energetically against reformism with its treacherous ideology and practice. Therefore, it is the duty of the workers' class to continue and step up its criticism of the reformists who, following their theory of the "parliamentary way to socialism," cannot and do not want to use the parliament in the fight against the capitalists and refuse to mobilize, organize and utilize the people's masses against the counter-revolutionary bourgeoisie.

The fight against the opportunists who are unable to drop their policy of cooperation and compromise with the capitalists and landowners, whether they are aware of it or not, cannot be separated from a systematic and purposeful effort to establish cooperation and to create a unity of action with Social Democratic and other socialist parties. This has been made possible by the change of objective and subjective processes in the world during this present historical epoch. The struggle for the preservation of national independence, democracy, peace and the betterment of the social position of the working people presents itself, under present conditions, increasingly as a common task of Communist and all other political parties and organizations which acknowledge the principles of socialism and democracy. In the present situation, not the questions of fundamental differences should be emphasized but those questions which are common and which reflect immediate interests.

Evidence of the possibility and success of such a struggle is again to be found in our own experience. In the course of the fight against the occupiers and their helpers among the big bourgeoisie in this country, in the course of the fight for the recovery of national and state independence and of the antifascist fight for democratic right of the people, a broad National Front of workers, peasants, tradesmen, intelligentsia and part of bourgeoisie was created. This National Front, headed by the workers' class, represented a decisive internal force ensuring the victory of the national and democratic revolution.

The Creation of a Socialist Bloc

The unity of action of the workers' class and the strong influence of the ideas of socialism, manifesting itself in the course of the national and democratic revolution, made it possible to conclude, in June 1945, within the framework of the National Front, a "socialist bloc." The creation of the socialist bloc within the National Front signified an agreement between the CPCS, the CS Social Democratic Party and the CS National Socialist Party on a common advance in all questions resulting from the execution of the Kosice government program. The existence of the "socialist bloc," whose representatives were in the majority in government, could signify the possibility of a relatively fast transition to socialism while a continuous strengthening of left and truly socialist elements in the non-Communist parties was proceeding. The practice and development of the forces in the country has shown, however, that the main significance of the agreement was the fact that this agreement, concluded before the eyes of rank-and-file members of the parties concerned, strengthened the unity of the workers' class and made it more difficult for the bourgeoisie and its agents in the leadership of the National Socialist and Social Democratic parties to find a way out of the obligation to execute the government program which had become the political foundation of the bloc. (It fulfilled the tactical principle of obtaining from all unreliable allies concessions, obligations and promises as far-reaching as possible, this being the surest way to compromise them and to help the faithful allies within these parties. This device and this form of cooperation may lead in another situation in other countries to a gradual rapprochement between the socialist parties and this to far greater and deeper consequences.) Both these agreements and this cooperation — the creation of the National Front with the representatives of other political parties and the creation of the "socialist bloc" — were and could be effected only because they came into being under the pressure of the unity of popular masses, their actual cooperation from "below."

The whole course of the struggle in the years 1945-1948 demonstrated that the decisive and basic factor in creating and strengthening the action unity of the workiers' class is its creation from "below" in the course of the fight for immediate political, economic and social demands of the working people. Thus, for instance, when in 1947 the Communists put forward in the government the demand of a "Millionaires' Levy" for the benefit of the peasants suffering through the consequences of a catastrophic drought, even the representatives of the Social Democratic Party raised their voice against this demand. The Communists immediately organized a common stand and pressure by the popular masses, especially a common and resolute stand of the workers' class, for the approval of this demand. "Rude Pravo," the central organ of the CPCS, published immediately after the refusal to approve the "Millionaires' Levy" the names of all the ministers who voted against the measure and added the following disclosure: "All these gentlemen were elected by our people in the honest belief that they have subscribed to the program of the National Front. However, by their attitude, they demonstrated to the broad masses of workers, peasants, office workers and tradesmen who elected them that they protect millionaires, speculators, industrialists, landowners and merchants. There are only 35,000 such people in our country. Their votes would hardly suffice for two mandates. In fact, they found supporters in the four parties of the National Front in the government." ("Rude Pravo," 4.10.57.)

This comprehensive and clear demand of the Communists brought the rank and file members of the Social Democratic Party into the common fight against the right wing forces in their own party: Organizations as a whole stood resolutely behind the common actions. This represented a very strong pressure on the leadership of the Social Democratic Party, a weakening of the right wing and strengthening of the left, with the result that after a week's struggle, on September 11, an agreement was concluded between the leadership of the CPCS and the leadership of the Social Democratic party on common action. This agreement contained very important obligations on both sides:

1. to submit a common draft proposal for the "Millionaires' Levy";
2. to proceed jointly in the question of remuneration of state employees;
3. to fight for the unity of the National Front and to appeal to the membership of both parties to act in unity from "below."

From Democracy, to Socialism, to Marxism

This whole tactic offers a clear example of the decisive influence of unity at the bottom upon the possibility of effective cooperation with the leadership of other socialist parties. This tactic which the Communists employed during the whole period 1945-1948, i.e., during the period of transition from national and democratic revolution to socialist revolution, led to a strengthening and greater decisiveness on the left wing of the Social Democratic Party and to its successive shift to the positions of true revolutionary Marxism and, thus, to its gradual ideological harmony with the Communists. It prepared conditions for the left wing of the Social Democratic Party to expel right-wing representatives from the party at the moment when the right, reformist wing prepared for an open crossing to the side of the bourgeoisie (in the February crisis in 1948), to cleanse the party and to increase substantially the party's co-operation with the Communists.

Our experience with the creation of an action unity of the workers' class, one of the fundamental conditions of a peaceful transition to socialism, shows that the center of its true beginning must be pressure from below, systematic uncovering of the reformist theory and of cooperation with the bourgeoisie, a common fight of the broad masses of all socialist parties or parties and organizations approving the revolutionary demands of the working people; in other words, direct actions from below based on our own experience of fighting and winning.

The Soviet Model

Apart from this, the practical experience of the Czechoslovak way to socialism confirmed the validity of many basic experiences of the Great October Revolution. In these basic, generally valid experiences of socialist revolution, the Soviet Union stands as an example for all; thus, in spite of its specific aspects, our revolution has taken its course and follows basically the way taken by the Soviet Union. It is a very important task, also, from the point of view of the international workers' movement and its needs, to analyze how far the generally valid principles of socialist building are applied under the concrete historical conditions prevailing in our country. All our experiences must be scientifically classified; it must be shown under what situations and conditions they originated and the process of their materialization must be demonstrated.

Our example has shown that Czechoslovakia's transition to the building of socialism was successful only because it was under the political direction of the workers class headed by the Marxist-Leninist Czechoslovak Communist Party. It has shown that the specific form of transition did not affect in any way the substance of the new force created by the socialist revolution, the dictatorship of the proletariat. It confirmed the validity of Lenin's maxim saying that every nation advancing towards socialism "will add something specific to any existing form of democracy, to any existing form of dictatorship of the proletariat, to any concrete pace of socialist transformation of the various aspects of social life." (Lenin's Works, CS edition 1957, page 71.)

While the tasks and the form of the dictatorship of the proletariat established by the proletariat in the October Socialist Revolution corresponded to the actual historical situation in Russia and to the contemporary relationship of internal and international class forces, the tasks and the form of the dictatorship of the proletariat in people's democratic Czechoslovakia correspond to the actual historical situation in Czechoslovakia. This form of the dictatorship of the proletariat differs by a number of points from the form adopted by the October Socialist Revolution:

- By the existence of the National Front as a political expression of unity between the workers' class and the working peasantry and the other working people;

- By the existence of more political parties within the framework of the National Front. These non-Communist political parties are, in their substance, petty-bourgeois parties, fully recognizing, however, and subordinating themselves to, the leadership of the CPCS and serving the building of socialism and the common fight of the people for peace;

- By the recognition of former bourgeois parliamentary institutions, such as the parliament, president, etc., which have, however, adopted a new, socialist purpose;

- By not depriving the bourgeoisie of the right to vote, having adopted the principle of universal, secret and direct ballot. Our way has supplied a definite proof that Marxism-Leninism has nothing in common with a "cult of violence" and has shaken very seriously the lying propaganda of reformism, attempting to persuade the working masses that the basic difference between the revolutionary workers' movement and reformism lies in the question of a "non-bloody" way to socialism. The violence employed by the Great Socialist October Revolution was forced upon the proletariat of Russia by Russian and international bourgeoisie. This violence of the Great Socialist October Revolution, was therefore, only a necessary, specific aspect corresponding to the historical situation, and not a generally valid rule of a socialist revolution.

In 1919, in the midst of a grave civil war in Russia and in the days of the foundation of the Hungarian Soviet Republic, V. I. Lenin proclaimed:

> "In a state in which the bourgeoisie do not offer such furious resistance, the situation for Soviet power will be easier; it will be able to work there without violence, without the bloody way forced upon us by Messrs. Kerensky and the imperialists . . . Other countries arrive at the same goal, Soviet power, by another, more human way . . . The example given by Russia alone was not fully understandable to the workers everywhere in the world. They knew that there were Soviets in Russia; they all were for the Soviets, but they were frightened by the horrors of the

> bloody fight. The example of Hungary will be decisive for the proletarian masses, for the European proletariat and for the working peasants." (V. I. Lenin: "Works," vol. 29, CS edition, 1955, page 264, 265.)

Also, a "cult of violence'' cannot be followed by the workers' class, because a violent armed fight is not at all advantageous to it from the point of view of its aim — the achievement of a complete socialist revolution. This aim combines two inseparable tasks: to oust the power of the bourgeoisie and to organize a new, higher method of social production, to organize and build socialism. The latter task is more serious and more difficult, for it is the greatest source of strength required for the definite victory over the bourgeoisie, a source of firmness and steadfastness of the dictatorship of the proletariat.

It is just this more difficult and serious, more decisive task that the workers' class can fulfil much faster with the help of peace production forces, without a civil war — which is unthinkable — without disorganization of the country, destruction of production forces, without the sacrifice of the best cadres of the workers' class which, instead of following the slogan, "All for the fastest socialist transformation of the country," must execute the slogan "All for the victory on the civil war front."

When V. I. Lenin evaluated the reasons for the imperialist intervention in the Great Socialist October Revolution and its consequences, he pointed to the following fact:

> "The West European capitalist powers did everything possible, partly on purpose, partly spontaneously, to throw us back and to use the civil war in Russia for the greatest possible devastation of the country. It was just this out-

come of the imperialist war which had considerable advantages for them: if the revolutionary order in Russia could not be extirpated, then, at least, the progress toward socialism could be retarded. This was the way in which these powers were thinking, and from their point of view they could have hardly thought differently. In actual fact they reached the aim half way. They did not destroy the new order brought about by the revolution but they did prevent it from making such progress that would confirm the correctness of socialist predictions enabling the socialists to expand rapidly the production forces and to develop all those possibilities which form the basis of socialism, to prove to the whole world clearly what enormous forces are hidden in socialism and that humanity was now entering a new stage of development with extraordinary and splendid opportunities." (V. I. Lenin: "Works", vol. 23, CS edition, 1955, p. 498.)

The Czechoslovak example is evidence that an apparently slower progress of socialist revolution (by gradual transition of national and democratic revolution into a socialist revolution) was actually the faster way, because the two-in-one task of the socialist revolution began to be fulfilled simultaneously. While fast removal of the consequences of war, efforts to renew quickly production forces, economic progress of the country, a new working discipline, advance of education and culture, were at first aimed at the total political defeat of the bourgeoisie, all these efforts, in their consequence, created simultaneously the main conditions of a faster and more definite securing of power in the hands of the working class. In February 1948, i.e., at the time when the workers' class had already achieved all political power and when the people's democracy was realized as a state of the dictatorship of the proletariat,

(a) the state apparatus was already in existence in principle and the working class could use it in its fight for socialism;
(b) the first important successes had already been achieved in creating a new working discipline and a new relationship to work;
(c) the working masses had already gained experience in state, organizational and educational work;
(d) new forms of organization of working people were in existence, as required for leading the broad popular masses in socialist building; these new forms represented an important part of the system of the dictatorship of the proletariat following a complete assumption of power by the working class;
(e) the economy of the country, disrupted by the war, was already rehabilitated in principle.

All this is created and achieved by the proletariat only after its victory, if violent attainment of socialism through civil war must be chosen. This is truly convincing evidence that a "cult of violence" is absolutely unacceptable for Marxist-Leninist parties because it is in conflict with their fundamental needs and aims. The confirmation of this principle by the actual course of our revolution has greatly enhanced the attraction of socialism.

The Czech Example: Building Proletarian Internationalism

In appraising our experiences and our contribution to the international workers' movement this must not be forgotten. The possibility of the peaceful progress of socialist revolution making revolutionary use of the parliament, as pointed our by the

20th Congress of the Soviet CP, is a product of new class conditions created by far-reaching objective and subjective changes in the world. It is a product of class consequences resulting from the existence of the world socialist system and its political, economic and ideological strength. People's democratic Czechoslovakia, as one of the most highly industrialized states in the world, is a very important part of this system. The fast industrial expansion and the growing standard of living in people's democratic Czechoslovakia take a direct part, through their consequences, in the changes in objective and subjective processes in the world, processes weakening capitalism and strengthening socialism. They take an active part in the creation of conditions in which the possibility of the peaceful advancement of socialist revolution exists and in which it can be materialized. The working people of Czechoslovakia, like the working masses in all countries of the world socialist system, have the good fortune that their building and their systematic raising of the living standard also promote the concrete purpose of their proletarian internationalism. Through their successes, they prepare the ground for the Communist parties, for the workers' classes and for the broad masses in the capitalist countries and countries dependent upon them for a peaceful transition to socialism with the help of the Parliament. (The example of Hungary demonstrates how every success, and every failure, exerts a direct and deep influence on the formation of the fundamental force for this transition — on the formation of a broad united popular front on the winning over of new allies of the workers' class.)

Such is and must be our contribution, an unusually valuable and instructive contribution, to the international workers' movement, a contribution to the creation of conditions favorable to an accelerated march of the world proletarian revolution.

Index

About Robert Welch University Press ...

This new edition of *And Not A Shot Is Fired* is an edifying successor to *Philip Dru: Administrator* — the premier book-length publication of Robert Welch University Press. In the Foreword to *Philip Dru*, journalist William Norman Grigg described that novel (written by Woodrow Wilson's "alter ego," Edward Mandell House) as being an essential part of any political science student's collection of "political works which are read primarily for precautionary reasons."

Though published as a work of fiction in 1912, *Philip Dru* served as a clear blueprint for the heinous "isms" of the middle part of this century that drew the world into two world wars, and coerced a substantial portion of the earth's population into living under totalitarian collectivism.

And Not A Shot Is Fired is a case study of the effects of such machinations on a single country — Czechoslovakia. Thomas R. Eddlem notes in its Foreword: "This document is a 'how-to' manual for totalitarian takeover of an elected parliamentary system of government through mainly *legal* and *constitutional* means." Kozak and his co-conspirators manipulated the Czechoslovak people into voting themselves into slavery by using what he called "pressure from above" and "pressure from below."

But why should a busy modern American set aside the time to read this brief history of an extinct state? The reason is that the same tactics described in Kozak's book are in wide use today, by other conspirators. As former Czechoslovakian Vice-Premier Petr Zenkl warned: "Read it and heed it, gentlemen of the Free World, while you are free."

The administrators of RWU Press do not take lightly the responsibility of making revealing studies of this caliber readily available to all students, instructors, and devotees of political science and public affairs. (Or at least to those sufficiently inspired to approach these studies from a perspective of true intellectual fervor, curiosity and, we would hope, a commitment to improve the human condition.)

In selecting titles for publication, the editors of RWU Press shall be guided by a philosophy of respect for intellectual, historical, and ethical truth — rather than by the current trend of "political correctness." For the former is perennial, the latter is transitory.

"There is one thing a professor can be absolutely certain of," noted University of Chicago professor Allan Bloom in *The Closing of the American Mind*, "almost every student entering the university believes, or says he believes, that truth is relative.... The relativity of truth is not a theoretical insight but a moral postulate, the condition of a free society, or so they see it. They have all been equipped with this framework early on, and it is the modern replacement for the inalienable natural rights that used to be the traditional American grounds for a free society.... Openness used to be the virtue that permitted us to seek the good by using reason. It now means accepting everything and denying reason's power." It is "not a means to exploring different answers to the great questions, but an excuse not to try to answer them at all."

Robert Welch University Press will not flee from its self-assigned mission to explore "different answers to the great questions."

The most pressing question of all, in the context of American society on the eve of the Twenty-first Century, is: How can we preserve, defend, and export America's greatest commodity: a legacy of political freedom in which all other freedoms — cultural, religious, economic, and academic — will flourish?